TOWARD A NEW NATIONALISM

SECOND EDITION

GREG JOHNSON

Counter-Currents Publishing Ltd.
San Francisco
2023

Cover image: Johannes Vermeer, *The Geographer*, 1668–1669

Cover design by Kevin I. Slaughter

Published in the United States by
COUNTER-CURRENTS PUBLISHING LTD.
http://www.counter-currents.com/

Hardcover ISBN: 978-1-64264-025-0
Paperback ISBN: 978-1-64264-026-7
E-book ISBN: 978-1-64264-027-4

CONTENTS

PREFACE

Toward a New Nationalism is a companion volume to
The White Nationalist Manifesto. Many of the essays in
the sections on White Nationalism and the Jewish question were written for the *Manifesto* but dropped to make
the book shorter and more focused. The essays in the
section on the Alt Right chronicle its rise and fall,
spelling out lessons to be learned for the next chapter of
white identity politics.

This second edition drops two sections of essays, one
on the "Deep State," the other on particular individuals.
It also drops six of the more journalistic essays on the Alt
Right. But it also adds an essay, "It's Okay to Be White."
These changes make the book shorter and more unified.
Thus I hope it will also be more impactful.

I wish to thank the publisher and translator of the
French edition of this book for suggesting the new table
of contents.[1] I also wish to thank John Morgan and Michael Polignano for helping bring this book to press;
Kevin Slaughter for his work on the cover for both editions; the many readers who submitted ideas and images
for the cover; Alex Graham for help with the index for
both editions; and F. Roger Devlin, Tom Goodrich, and
Richard McCulloch for their promotional quotes

I also wish to thank Jez Turner of the London Forum,
Fróði Midjord of the Scandza Forum, Stead Steadman of
the Jonathan Bowden Dinner, and the organizers of
Erkenbrand and the Finnish Awakening Conference for
inviting me to give six talks included here.

Finally, I wish to thank the many writers, donors, and

---

[1] Greg Johnson, *Vers un nouveau nationalisme,* trans. Pascal
Jordan (London: White Revolution Books, 2023).

commenters at Counter-Currents who made it all possible.

The original edition of this book was dedicated to my friend Charles Wing Krafft, who had just survived surgery for cancer. The cancer returned, and two years later, he died. This edition is dedicated to his memory.

June 25, 2023

WHY RACE IS NOT A
SOCIAL CONSTRUCT

Race realism is one of the intellectual foundations of White Nationalism. Race realism is the thesis that racial differences are *objective facts of nature*, which pre-exist human consciousness, human society, and even the human race itself—since there were different species and subspecies before mankind emerged.

Nature must be understood in contrast to *conventions*—like human languages and laws—which do not exist independent of human consciousness and society.

As objective facts of nature, racial differences cannot be safely ignored. Nor can natural racial differences be transformed simply by altering legal or linguistic conventions. Conventions can only alter racial realities by guiding human action to change nature itself. For instance, if we institute eugenic or dysgenic incentives, this will change the genes of future generations.

The opposite of race realism is the idea of the "social construction of race," the thesis that racial differences are not objective facts but rather shared social conventions, which may vary from time to time and from place to place, like languages and table manners.

The social construction of race is one of the intellectual foundations of racial egalitarianism, for if race is socially constructed, then so is racial inequality. This offers the possibility that racial inequality can be replaced with equality simply by altering social conventions, like laws and language.

THE BASIS OF RACE REALISM

The basis of race realism is sense experience. Different races *appear* different from one another. Different subraces appear different from one another. Racially mixed children appear different from pure specimens. Even races that appear superficially similar—like Australian aborigines and African blacks—appear to be different on closer inspection. Careful observers do not confuse the two. Racial differences are not just a matter of "skin color," but of morphology and behavior as well, both of which can be observed empirically.[1]

Note that I do not claim that racial realism is based in *science*. People were aware of racial differences long before the emergence of science. Science comes along only later, to explain observable racial differences. Scientific theories are, moreover, verified or falsified based on their ability to explain observed racial differences. Observable racial differences are, therefore, the Alpha and the Omega of racial science. Thus the foundation of race realism is sense experience, not scientific theorizing.

This is important to understand, because it implies that problems with *theories* of race do not in any way alter the *perceptible differences* between races.

It is also important to understand that race realism is the default, common-sense position of all mankind. We observe differences between races, subraces, and hybrids—human and otherwise—before we learn words to communicate and classify them, and before we create theories to explain them.

I vividly remember my first experience of a non-white: a waiter in the dining car of a train. I was 4 or 5 years old. I was especially taken by the contrast in color between the

---

[1] An excellent basic textbook on race distinguished in terms of observable, morphological features that remains valid to this day is Carleton S. Coon, *The Living Races of Man* (New York: Random House, 1965). The book is particularly valuable for its many photographs illustrating typical racial, subracial, and hybrid types.

back and the front of the man's hands. When he went away, I asked my mother what I had seen, and she told me that he was not just a white man turned brown, but a different kind of man called a "Negro." But I already *saw* the differences before I was *told* the name and explanation. Indeed, I asked for an explanation *because* I saw the differences. My mother and I certainly did not construct the differences that were apparent to all.

Given that race realism is the default, common-sense position, proponents of social constructivism need to offer arguments for their claim. In this essay, I criticize four arguments for the social construction of race, which I characterize as follows: (1) the argument from the social construction of knowledge in general; (2) the argument from changing racial classifications; (3) the argument from continua; and (4) the argument from the silence of science. This is not an exhaustive list, nor is this a "scholarly" survey and critique.[2] I chose these arguments simply because they are commonly used in middle-brow online debates. I conclude by treating the thesis of the social construction of race as a social construct itself, exposing the political agenda and power relations behind social constructivism.

1. THE SOCIAL CONSTRUCTION OF KNOWLEDGE IN GENERAL

One argument for the social construction of race is a simple deduction from the general thesis that "All knowledge is socially constructed." This is a philosophical thesis about the relationship between mind and reality, which holds that there is no single correct account of any aspect of reality, but rather a plurality of equally valid accounts which are relative to the contingent circumstances

---

[2] For a more comprehensive survey of the case for race realism and against social constructivism, see Richard McCulloch, "Race: Reality and Denial," *The Occidental Quarterly*, vol. 2, no. 4 (Winter 2002–2003): 5–26.

of different communities. For instance, there is the scientific account of the origin of the species, and there is the Biblical account, both of which are products of different communities, and there is no neutral standpoint or criterion that allows us to claim that one approach is better or truer than another.

I believe that this sort of relativism is philosophically incoherent in itself.[3] But it also fails as a justification of the social construction of race because, in a sense, it proves too much. For if everything is a social construct, the concept loses all utility. Social construction only makes sense if there is a contrast term, namely objective natural facts.

But if everything is a social construct, then we have to ask: Is the social construct *race* more like the social construct *money* or the social construct *gravity*? Because it is in society's power to change money, but it is not in our power to change gravity. A philosopher who defends the idea that gravity is a social construct still leaves the lecture hall by the door rather than the window because he knows that one ignores some social constructs at one's own risk.

The social constructivist clearly wants race to be like money rather than gravity, but if everything is a social construct, he needs to offer an additional argument to prove that racial inequalities can be abolished by social fiat.

2. CHANGING RACIAL CLASSIFICATIONS

One of the most common arguments for the social construction of race is along the following lines: (1) If racial differences are real, then racial classification schemes will not vary from time to time and place to place. (2) Ra-

---

[3] See Paul Boghossian, *Fear of Knowledge: Against Relativism and Constructivism* (Oxford: Clarendon, 2007).

cial classification schemes vary from time to time and place to place. For instance, the same mixed-race individual might be considered black or white in different places and at different times.[4] Therefore, racial differences are not real. And, since racial differences are either real or social constructs, they must be social constructs.

This argument has two main problems.

The first premise is simply false because it elides the distinction between reality and opinion. Racial differences can be perfectly real, but people's *opinions* about racial differences can vary widely. Since human beings are fallible, there can be many opinions about one and the same fact. But that does not make the facts any less objective. It just proves that people frequently fail to be as objective as the facts.

The oft-cited example of varying standards of blackness proves nothing about racial realities. First, the very idea of categorizing mixed-race individuals as black or white is problematic, simply because they are mixed. Given that they are neither black nor white, it is not surprising that people make different decisions if they have to classify them as one or the other. Thus it may be arbitrary social convention to say that Barack Obama is a black man. But it is an objective fact of nature that he had a white mother and a black father and is therefore half white and half black.

3. CUTTING THE CONTINUUM

Another common argument for the social construction of race, and of knowledge in general, depends on the distinction between differences of *degree* and differences of *kind*, and runs as follows. (1) If racial differences are real differences of kind, then there should not be a continuum

---

[4] Ta-Nehisi Coates, "What We Mean When We Say 'Race Is a Social Construct,'" *The Atlantic*, May 15, 2013.

of intermediate types. (2) There are continuua of intermediate types between races. Therefore, there is only one
human race, and distinctions between races are not found
in nature but constructed by human beings. We carve up
the continuum. Nature does not come separated into different kinds.[5]

There are two major problems with this argument.

The first premise strikes me as highly dubious: Just because there are continua in nature does not mean that
there are no real distinctions between parts of a given
continuum. In terms of color, red may shade off into orange, and different cultures might have different words for
colors and make finer or grosser distinctions between
them. But does this mean that there are no real, observable differences between, say, red and blue?

Evolutionary theory posits the common origin and evolutionary continuity of all life on earth. Does that continuity mean, therefore, that there are no real differences between mammals and birds, or birds and reptiles, or nematodes and human beings? Is the difference between dinosaurs and humans merely a "social construct"? Did dino-

---

[5] An underlying assumption of this argument is that to truly know objective reality, the mind must be passive and reality
must simply inscribe itself upon it. Thus if the mind is in any
way active in the process of gaining knowledge, we no longer
know objective reality but only human constructs. Ayn Rand
offers a *reductio ad absurdum* of this argument, although she
mistakenly applies it to Kant: "[Kant's] argument, in essence,
ran as follows: man is *limited* to a consciousness of a specific
nature, which perceives by specific means and no others,
therefore, his consciousness is not valid; man is blind, because
he has eyes—deaf, because he has ears—deluded, because he
has a mind—and the things he perceives do not exist, *because*
he perceives them." Ayn Rand, "For the New Intellectual," in
For the New Intellectual: The Philosophy of Ayn Rand (New
York: Random House, 1961), p. 33.

saurs not exist before human beings were around to "socially construct" them?

If race is a social construct, is the human race as a whole a "social construct" too? What then is society? What is society made up of *before* the social construction of the human race? Is society also a social construct, which would seem to get us into an infinite regress (society is a social construct of a social construct of a social construct . . .)? Or is society not a social construct? Is it just a fact of nature? Is it just *here*? Then why can't other things be facts of nature, like human beings and dinosaurs?

The second premise is also problematic. Anthropologists claim that all human races descend from common ancestors. But at different points in time, the five distinct human races—Caucasoid, Mongoloid, Congoid, Capoid, and Australoid—branched off and differentiated themselves from both their common ancestors and one another. After developing in isolation for enough time to attain distinctive traits, these races then came into contact with one another and gave rise to mixed populations.[6] But the existence of racially mixed individuals no more overthrows the real distinction between races than the existence of green paint refutes the existence of blue and yellow paint.[7]

4. THE SILENCE OF SCIENCE

Another common claim of the social constructivists is that science does not give adequate support to the idea of real racial distinctions, thus social constructivism is true. The argument runs as follows. (1) If there are real racial

---

[6] For an accessible account of racial evolution that remains valid today, see Carleton S. Coon, *The Origin of Races* (New York: Knopf, 1962). See also Coon's *The Living Races of Man*.

[7] John R. Baker makes this point in his *Race* (New York: Oxford University Press, 1974), p. 100.

differences, then science will explain them. (2) Science has not explained racial differences. Therefore, there are no real racial differences. Since racial differences are either real or socially constructed, race is a social construct.

This argument has four grave problems.

First, race realism is based on observed racial differences, not on scientific theories of race. Human beings perceived racial differences long before the emergence of science, and we perceive them still, even those of us who are entirely innocent of racial science (as most social constructivists happen to be). Thus the first premise is simply false: The *reality* of race does not depend on the success or failure of scientific *theories* of race. Theories may rise and fall, but observable differences remain.

As for the second premise: Scientists would beg to differ.[8] We can determine the race of an individual from the morpoholgical or genetic analysis of a single bone or strand of hair.

Of course, the social constructivists are not exactly clear about what constitutes the failure of science to explain race, but they generally insinuate that science has either (1) failed to come up with a single differentiating trait possessed by all members of a race and not possessed by other races,[9] or (2) that no such theory has attained universal acceptance.

But the demand for a single essential differentiating trait for each race is arbitrary. Nature does not have to conform to our demands. And the fact that a theory does not attain universal acceptance has nothing to do with its

---

[8] For a simple and compelling summary of the science of race, see J. Philippe Rushton, *Race, Evolution, and Behavior: A Life History Perspective*, 2nd special abridged edition (Port Huron, Michigan: Charles Darwin Research Institute, 2000).

[9] See Joseph L. Graves, Jr., "The Biological Case against Race," *American Outlook*, Spring 2002, p. 31.

truth, given the variability and fallibility of human opinions. Frankly, I believe that most social constructivists are intellectually dishonest. Thus no theory of objective racial differences will ever gain universal assent, no matter how well founded it may be.

Another problem with this argument is that it overlooks the fact that science is a process that unfolds over time. Thus even if the second premise were true, the conclusion does not follow, simply because science might not have come up with the correct account *just yet*. But wait.

A final problem with this argument is its assumption that in the absence of a scientific explanation of race, the only alternative is social constructivism. In fact, the default position is race realism based on empirical observation, which does not depend upon scientific explanation at all.

SOCIAL CONSTRUCTIVISM AS SOCIAL CONSTRUCT

Social constructivists typically do not limit their thesis to race. Many claim that all knowledge is a social construct, or even that reality itself is a social construct. Thus it is fair to ask: Is social constructivism itself a social construct? If social constructivism is a social construct, this has three important implications:

1. Like all social constructs, social constructivism is the product of a unique set of historically contingent circumstances.
2. Since every society is divided into the rulers and the ruled, every social construct will be marked by the agenda of those who hold power.
3. If social constructivism is a social construct, not a natural fact, its acceptance or rejection is not based on reason and nature but on social incentives: moral and political commitment for

the true believers—brainwashing, greed, and
fear for the rest.

Social constructivism has a long philosophical pedi-
gree, but today it functions as the metaphysical postulate
of egalitarian social engineering projects to equalize the
races by revolutionizing European founded and dominat-
ed societies. Of course, this revolution cannot produce
racial equality, but it can create a new racial hierarchy in
which Europeans are subordinate. Social constructivism
thus serves the interests of a new emerging social elite, an
alliance of rootless plutocrats, non-whites, sexual minorities, and other outsiders, in which the organized Jewish
community is the senior and guiding partner. Thus social
constructivism is an element of what Kevin MacDonald
calls the "culture of critique": the critique and overthrow
of European civilization by Jewish-inspired and dominat-
ed intellectual movements like Marxism, psychoanalysis,
the Frankfurt School, feminism, deconstructionism, and
most forms of postmodernism.[10]

These movements are characterized by pseudo-science,
obscurantism, and crass ethno-political advocacy. They
acquired their influence not through reason and science
but through the subversion of the educational, cultural,
and political institutions of European societies. They per-
petuate their influence though the indoctrination of the
impressionable and the suppression of dissent.

Thus social constructivism cannot be defeated merely
by criticizing its astonishingly poor arguments, which in
large part are merely tools of self-conscious and cynical
deception. If you lop off one argument, the hydra just

---

[10] Kevin MacDonald, *The Culture of Critique: An Evolutionary Analysis of Jewish Involvement in Twentieth-Century Intellectual and Political Movements* (Westport, Conn.: Praeger,
1998).

sprouts another.

Instead, social constructivism must be defeated on its own terms: by altering the social conditions that give rise to it, by changing who rules this society, by disempowering and silencing its advocates just as they disempower and silence their critics. In short, social constructivism must be socially deconstructed and replaced by a new cultural and political hegemony that is aligned with reason, reality, and white interests. And we can do that in good conscience, because social constructivism is a false and pernicious ideology, nothing more.

Race realism is the default position of common sense. It is, moreover, supported by the best biological science. There is no good case for the social construction of race. It would be truer to say that society is a racial construct, meaning that society is the creation of human beings, who exist as part of nature and whose biological traits shape and constrain society and culture.

But once society is established, social conventions shape the underlying race by instituting eugenic and dysgenic breeding incentives or simply by legislating the extermination of entire groups. Nature comes before culture, but once culture exists, it turns back on and modifies nature.[11] Only in this specific sense can one say that race is a (partial) social "construct," although it would be better to drop the misleading language of construction altogether.

Counter-Currents, July 24, 2015

---

[11] For a recent and compelling account of genetic and cultural co-evolution, see Gregory Cochran and Henry Harpending, *The 10,000 Year Explosion: How Civilization Accelerated Human Evolution* (New York: Basic Books, 2009).

WHO ARE WE?
NORDICS, ARYANS, & WHITES

White Nationalism presupposes an answer to the question "Who is white?" White Nationalism is a political movement, whereas white identity is a metapolitical question. A precise answer to this question provides the foundation for effective white advocacy. False or imprecise answers, however, lead to confused and ineffective efforts. I wish to deal with two such misleading answers: "Nordicism" and "Aryanism." Both attitudes undermine White Nationalism by introducing confusions about white identity.

The archetypal Nordic is tall, long-headed, and fair-skinned, with blonde hair and blue eyes. Nordic types and traits are found throughout Europe, but as the name suggests, they are more prevalent in the North. As I define it, Nordicism is the view that the Nordic type is the model, paradigm, or archetype of whiteness, with the implication that non-Nordic is non-white, or white to a lesser degree. The most childish Nordicists actually imagine that the only way Europeans could acquire dark hair, eyes, and complexions is through racial admixture.

The Aryans were the creators of a particular language and culture. Their homeland, apparently, was in Eastern Europe, somewhere between the Baltic and Black Seas (an area now populated by Slavs and Balts, whom some Nordicists consider inferior breeds). In the second millennium BC, the Aryans began to migrate West into Europe, South into the Middle East, and East as far as India and China, diffusing their language, culture, and genes in the process. Because of the expanse of this diffusion, Aryans are also called Indo-Europeans. The original Aryans are thought to have been Nordic types, hence the same physical traits are described as Aryan and Nordic. Just as Nordicism regards the Nordic as archetypically white, the Aryanist makes Indo-European languages and cultures normative.

What's wrong with Nordicism? Nothing really, if one is a Nordic. It seems perfectly natural and healthy for Nordic people to prefer the company of genetically similar people. Indeed, the brain is hard-wired to do so. I am a Nordic type, and I am most comfortable in northern climes among Nordic people. Other things being equal, I would prefer a Nordic mate who shares my recessive traits and can help pass them on to the next generation. These attitudes would only be objectionable if I expected non-Nordics to share them as well. This would be to take a natural preference that is *relative* to a subracial group and turn it into an *absolute* standard for all groups.

I don't even object to the idea of Nordic superiority. If groups really are different, then every group is bound to be objectively better than others *by some standards*. But we must remember that this also implies that the same groups are bound to be inferior *by other standards*. Nordics are objectively superior at creating prosperous, egalitarian, high-trust, low-corruption societies. As a Nordic, I am most comfortable in such societies, and many other peoples are attracted to such societies, if only as sponges and plunderers.

Nordics, however, are proving objectively inferior at preserving our societies due to low ethnocentrism, high trust, and extreme credulity in the face of predatory tribal peoples out to dispossess us. Nordic superiority becomes objectionable only if (1) we assume that Nordic excellences are the *only* criteria for judging societies, and (2) we forget that Nordics are not superior in everything.

Although such White Nationalists as Wilmot Robertson and William Pierce were strongly Nordicist, and their attitudes linger on, in my experience Nordic White Nationalists are the most aware of the weaknesses of our own people. Beyond that, the Nordics that have the most naïve and ingrained supremacist attitudes tend to be the liberals and Leftists who believe that non-white immigrants *can* become citizens of Nordic societies, that they *want* to become citizens, and that apparently we don't even have to *try* to assimilate them, because the Nordic way of life is so intrinsically compelling that everyone would spontaneously and voluntarily want to adopt it (without, I might add, divesting themselves of their own ethnic identities, which are apparently only superficial matters of clothing and food anyway).

Nordicism is problematic for White Nationalists because it undermines cooperation and trust among different European groups. This damages the ability of White Nationalists to advocate for white interests in European colonial societies like the United States and Canada, which were peopled by many different European ethnic groups which are increasingly blended into new ethnic groups—the American, the Canadian, etc.—which are not entirely Nordic. In Europe itself, Nordicism also undermines the pan-European solidarity necessary to prevent European infighting and to unify Europe in the face of extra-European threats.

Imagine, for instance, the feelings of an American with Greek or Italian ancestry toward William Pierce's National Alliance if he read Pierce's *Who We Are*, in which he laments that the Nordic invaders of Greece mongrelized themselves with the indigenous *European* populations rather than exterminating them to keep their blood pure—an exterminationist agenda that he envisioned for the future in *The Turner Diaries*. Such attitudes follow logically from the premise that Nordics are the only authentic Europeans, which implies that non-Nordics are lesser men. The National Alliance accepted non-Nordics as members, but such people could legitimately ask if the organization could really take their money and represent their interests in good faith.

The idea that Nordics are authentically and archetypically white is simply an intellectual error.

- ❖ First, there is no reason to think that the first Europeans were Nordic.
- ❖ Second, even if the first Europeans were Nordic, there is no reason to suppose that all departures from the Nordic type represent a decline from the ideal.

Nordics are just one branch of the European family tree and are no more or less authentically European than any other branch.

Another error that is allied to Nordicism is what I call the son-in-law fallacy. Many whites operate on the assumption that the only truly white people are those they would have marry into their family. And since most people's attitudes about such matters are based on genetic similarity, the son-in-law fallacy is really just a form of unconscious sub-racial chauvinism. It is perfectly natural and healthy to want to marry people who are genetically similar, so one can more reliably pass on one's genes and culture to the next generation. But this does not imply that groups one would not wish to marry into are less European or less white.

Aryanism is an even more problematic attitude than Nordicism. Again, Aryanism is the view that Indo-European language and culture are normatively white. At its most childish, Aryanism leads to the false inference that Basques, Finns, Hungarians, and Estonians are "not white" because they do not speak Indo-European languages. Equally childish is the inference that non-European Caucasians (Persians, Armenians, Indians) are somehow "us" because they speak Indo-European languages. The *reductio ad absurdum* of Aryanism is a European who feels more kinship with Persians and Hindus than Hungarians or Finns because of common linguistic roots. Of course, due to colonialism there are also millions of Africans, Amerindians, and Asians who speak Indo-European languages and even carry European genes. Logically, the Aryanist should also prefer these people to Basques or Estonians, but let us hope they shrink back before this absurdity. Europeans can learn a great deal about our own pre-Christian language and culture through the study of Aryan offshoots among non-Europeans. But those who bear these languages and cultures today are still non-Europeans—not "us."

There is no reason to presume that Indo-European language and culture are normatively European. The Aryans were a branch of the European family that split off from the main stem, evolved a distinct language and culture in isolation for untold millennia, and then migrated back into the European heartland, as well as into the Near, Middle, and Far East.

The Aryans certainly contributed to European civilization, but they did not create it. Indeed, when the various waves of Aryans returned to Europe, they were rightly regarded as barbarians. They even regarded themselves as barbarians. Agriculture, ceramics, metal-working, written language, clocks, calendars, astronomy, irrigation, urban life, the wheel, refined arts and crafts, monumental architecture—all of these were pre-Aryan inventions. Europe's first high civilizations arose around the Mediterranean shore, not in the North. Their creators were subracially Mediterranean, not Nordic. The creators of the high civilizations of Mesopotamia were Caucasian, but they were probably no more European than the current residents of those lands. And when the Aryans diffused themselves throughout Europe and the Orient, they were awestruck by the superior civilizations they found and eagerly to assimilated them, culturally and genetically, until Aryans in the pure form became extinct.

Europeans today, culturally and genetically, are more or less composites of Aryans and pre-Aryans. Thus it is a form of false consciousness—of inauthenticity—to identify ourselves, individually or collectively, with the Aryans, an extinct people who live on only as genetic and cultural *ingredients* of modern Europeans. The Aryans are *part* of us, but they are not us. Dreaming that we are Aryans is like a dog dreaming that he is a wolf.

Who are we then? Who is white? Who is European? A simple but pragmatic answer is that we are the branch of the Caucasian race that has inhabited Europe since the last Ice Age, as well as their unmixed descendants around the globe. Pragmatically, this common ancestry embraces all groups that we recognize as Europeans, but also excludes the non-European Caucasians in the Middle East, the Caucasus Mountains, and Central and South Asia.

Europeans and non-European Caucasians apparently had common ancestors. But when I speak of the European or white race, I am referring to the subset of the Caucasian race that settled and developed in Europe. Although there are liminal cases where the two sub-races blended, non-European Caucasians are culturally and genetically distinct from Europeans. Furthermore, non-European Caucasians exist in vast numbers and unlike Europeans, they are in no danger of extinction. Although breeding between European and non-Europeans Caucasians is not race-mixing in the strict sense, it should still be discouraged, since it erodes the genetic distinctness of an already threatened race.

If Nordicists think this definition includes people they would not want to live or breed with, they need not do so as long as they maintain their own distinct homelands.

Whites are united by a common origin, common enemies, and a common threat of extinction. The only common thing we lack is a way to prevent our complete genetic and cultural oblivion. The purpose of White Nationalism is to give our race a future again. Changing the course of history is no small task. It requires white consciousness and solidarity, as well as organization and world-historical action.

White solidarity need not conflict with particular regional, national, and sub-racial identities. Indeed, the whole purpose of White Nationalism is to *protect* such differences. But sub-racial and national *chauvinisms*— and imaginary identifications with extinct ancestors and non-Europeans who speak Indo-European languages— do conflict with the solidarity we need to save us. Nordicists and Aryanists are slated for destruction with all the rest of us. Which means that such attitudes are ultimately self-defeating. They are luxuries and indulgences a dying race can ill afford.

Counter-Currents, March 8, 2016

WHY CONSERVATIVES CONSERVE NOTHING

The White Nationalist critique of conservatives is simple: they conserve nothing. Therefore, we need to stop wasting our political time, energy, and money on conservatives and invest them in White Nationalism instead. And we need to do it immediately, while there is still something left to conserve.

Why do conservatives conserve nothing? Because to conserve anything, they have to win political power. Winning requires a conservative majority. Conservative voters tend to identify with their nation and its history, whereas Leftists tend to be alienated from it. In the United States and other white countries, it is natural that conservative voters are overwhelmingly white, whereas the Left tends to be a coalition of Jews, non-whites, and alienated whites (e.g., liberal ideologues, feminists, and sexual outliers).

White birthrates are below replacement levels in every country around the globe. If this trend continues, white countries will cease to exist. White populations will be replaced by growing non-white populations, whether through legal and illegal immigration or simply through the increase of non-white populations already within their borders. Even if a white country has secure borders and no non-whites, if its population declines enough, eventually burgeoning non-white populations will simply march in and make themselves at home. (While white populations decline worldwide, the population of black Africa is expected to double between now and 2050.)

As whites become minorities in our own homelands, it will be impossible for conservative politicians to win election. Therefore, it will be impossible to implement conservative policies. Therefore, the things that conservatives love will disappear. In the United States, that means limited constitutional government, fiscal responsibility, private enterprise, freedom of speech, freedom of religion, gun rights, etc. These values have tenuous enough footholds even in white countries and are almost non-existent in non-white countries.

In the short run, it might be possible for conservatives to hold onto power in certain localities and even to gain national office from time to time, due to unpredictable factors like wars, famines, scandals, and electoral whims. But in the long run, conservative policies will become politically impossible because the Left will have elected a new people with solidly Leftist preferences.

In short, conservatives will conserve nothing, because they will do nothing to preserve the white majorities needed to elect them.

At this point, conservatives will take another hit on the crack pipe of "minority outreach." They'll tell themselves that non-whites are "natural conservatives," even though there is precious little constitutionally limited government, fiscal responsibility, or individual freedom south of the Rio Grande, in Africa, or anywhere else where non-whites are the majority. They'll pander and cuck a little harder for the brown people. They'll put forward more black and Hispanic affirmative action candidates (Cain, Carson, Cruz, Rubio). They'll blubber and hope and pray that Jesus will miracle their asses into power for just once more election cycle. Anything, really, to avoid facing up to the slow, unrelenting countdown to white demographic Armageddon.

Of course white liberals are in the same boat. Both groups are aware that they are dying out. Neither group will lift a finger to stop the process. And when both groups contemplate the future of their values in a brown world, both of them pin everything on somehow converting their replacements, a kind of ideological transmigration from their enfeebled wraith-like bodies into the fecund, swarming colored masses. They never ask themselves why healthy races would want to adopt the values of a race that created the greatest political and economic orders in history, then consumed itself in self-indulgence, opened its borders, and gave everything away to peoples they should have held in contempt.

The only way for conservatives to conserve anything is first to conserve the white majority of natural conservatives. It can be done. White demographic decline is not a cosmic mystery. It is the predictable consequence of bad political decisions: affirmative action, feminism, desegregation, open borders, and economic globalization, for starters. It can be fixed by better decisions, starting with closing the borders; cutting illegal aliens off from employment, education, and social benefits; and then deporting the ones that do not self-deport.

Saving the white majority will be difficult. It becomes more difficult with each passing day. But it can be done, as I outline in my essay "Restoring White Homelands."[1] All we lack is political will. Why, then, are conservatives so opposed to doing the one thing that can save them and their values from long-term extinction? Why are they willing to gamble everything on the far more dubious and difficult path of converting a rising non-white majority to conservatism?

The answer is simple: Like a herd of elephants being stampeded off a cliff by a tiny mouse, conservatives are destroying themselves, their values, and their nations out of fear of a single word: "racism." Under the present dispensation, it is regarded as perfectly moral for Jews, blacks, Asians, Hispanics—everyone, really, except whites—to think

---

[1] Greg Johnson, "Restoring White Homelands," in *The White Nationalist Manifesto* (San Francisco: Counter-Currents, 2018).

of themselves as ethnic groups and to fight for their group interests in the political realm. For whites, however, that would be the sin of racism. And conservatives are willing to sin quite a lot—to lie, to break oaths, to betray their constituencies and their nations—but they'd rather die than be racist. They'd rather us die too, a decision that our enemies applaud.

Whites are allowed to think of ourselves only as human beings with generic human interests that by definition cannot conflict with those of other human beings. We can benefit as a group only by benefiting all humanity. This is the basis of the desperate conservative attempt to convert blacks and browns to the virtues of constitutional government and free enterprise, as if these are a race-neutral, universal ideology rather than specifically European cultural practices, which cannot be transplanted everywhere on the globe and cannot be sustained in our own homelands once we are replaced by non-whites.

Of course, conservatives are not above making crass appeals to the ethnic interests of non-whites. It is only white ethnic interests that are taboo. As I put it in my article, "The Conscience of a Cuckservative":

> By treating appeals to white ethnic interests as simply immoral, Republicans are . . . playing by rules dictated by the Democrats. And of course the Democrats have rigged the rules in their favor.
>
> Imagine American politics as a poker game. Each ethnic group has a place at the table and a certain number of chips, representing its collective wealth and power. Whites have the largest stack. But every group gets to play a wild card, "the race card," *except* for whites. No matter how big our initial advantage might be, if we play by those rules, we will lose hand after hand, until we have surrendered our wealth, our power, our country, and any

control we might have over our destiny—or we kick over the table and refuse to play a game rigged against us.[2]

I used to think conservatives were unprincipled. But they are highly principled. The problem is that their principles are provided by their enemies, and if we act upon them, we will be destroyed.

In America, however, the conservatives are getting worried. They were stung by the cuckservative barb; they are nervous about the rise of the Alt Right; and they are terrified of Donald Trump, who merely stands for a moderate, non-racial form of nationalism. But like their cousins the Social Justice Warriors, when their bullshit is called, conservatives just double down.

A case in point is David French's January 26, 2016 *National Review* article, "The Race-Obsessed Left has Released a Monster it Can't Control," which correctly argues that Left-wing, anti-white identity politics is giving rise to Right-wing, white identity politics (the "monster" in French's title).

French, however, is primarily concerned with keeping his hands clean of the taint of "racism." So he recommends that we ignore the fact that we are being attacked as whites and focus instead on "universal human dignity, with each of us created in the image of God." The trouble with such high-minded religious universalism is that it does not stop the onslaught of anti-white identity politics. It only numbs whites to the organized ethnic interest groups gnawing at our entrails.

As F. Roger Devlin argues so brilliantly in his essay "Why I Write":

---

[2] Greg Johnson, "The Conscience of a Cuckservative," *Truth, Justice, & a Nice White Country* (San Francisco: Counter-Currents, 2015).

Those traditional conservatives who continue to admonish us against the dangers of "biological determinism" are increasingly condemning themselves to irrelevance. The plea that "race isn't everything" is valid *per se*, but not especially germane to the situation in which we find ourselves. For we are not the aggressors in the battle now being fought. And in any battle, it is the aggressors' prerogative to choose the point of attack: if they come at you by land, you do not have the option of fighting them at sea.

Race *is* everything to our enemies, and it is the angle from which they have chosen to attack our entire civilization. It is also where they have achieved their greatest victories: you can see this from the way "conservative" groups feel they must parrot the language of the egalitarians just to get a hearing. Such well-meaning but naïve friends of our civilization are in effect consenting to occupy the status of a "kept" opposition.

The more we try to avoid confronting race directly, the more our enemies will press their advantage at precisely this point. Tactically, they are correct to do so. And they will continue until we abandon our defensive posture and turn to attack them on their own chosen ground.[3]

The great political battle of our time is over race and identity. Our enemies know it, but our friends don't. Conservatives conserve nothing because they won't fight. Whites are being attacked as a race. The conservative response, however, is to mumble something about universal human dignity and change the topic to ethanol subsidies.

---

[3] F. Roger Devlin, "Why I Write," *Counter-Currents*, November 10, 2010.

Whites can only defend ourselves as a race. We can only secure conservative values by conserving our race. We must embrace the politics of white racial identity. The only true conservatism is White Nationalism.

Counter-Currents, February 18, 2016

THE REFUTATION OF LIBERTARIANISM

This talk was delivered at the London Forum on October 3, 2015.

Libertarianism is the politics of individualism. Individualism is both a metaphysical and a moral position.

Metaphysical individualism is the thesis that only particular men exist. Groups are just collections of individuals, with no independent reality or meaning.

Metaphysical individualism is connected to universalism, which is the idea that there is only one race, the human race, which is just a collection of individuals. Universalism implies that there is no meaningful distinction between ingroups and outgroups, between us and them.

Universalism has two important implications.

First, since politics as Carl Schmitt defines it arises from the distinction between us and them, universalism implies that politics is merely a temporary phenomenon, based on the waning illusion of meaningful distinctions between ingroups and outgroups. When these distinctions disappear, politics will as well.

Second, nationalism, patriotism, and any other form of partiality for one's ingroup over an outgroup is morally illegitimate, since there is really no us and them, just me and you. This leads us to the ethical dimension of individualism. How do you and I get on together? If groups are just collections of individuals, there are no group values, just individual values. The purpose of social institutions, therefore, is to facilitate individuals pursuing their own aims.

The great facilitator of individuals pursuing their aims

is capitalism. If you and I have something to offer each other, we might trade. If we have nothing to offer each other, we just walk on by. The marketplace requires only a minimal "nightwatchman" state to protect us against force, fraud, breach of contract, and the like.

Ethical individualism requires us to treat individuals as individuals, not as members of various morally unimportant groups handed to us by history or nature. We must be "blind" to race. We must be "blind" to class. We must be "blind" to sex. We must be "blind" to religion. We must be "blind" to nationality. We must be "blind" to all things that divide us. The only thing we must see are individual merits.

The individualism game is highly advantageous for all players. Individualism unleashes creativity in science, technology, and business. But paradoxically, the greatest strength of individualism is the form of cooperation it fosters. Each individualist comports himself as a member of a potentially global society. This means that social cooperation can scale up to the global limit as well, making possible the wholesale transformation of the world we call modernity.

Collectivist societies, however, are hampered by ingroup/outgroup splits. If people behave as members of groups, trust and cooperation are confined to ingroups, which severely constricts the scale of social institutions and corrupts their functioning with favoritism toward ingroups and discrimination toward outgroups.

In honest contests, the individualist game can outcompete the collectivist game, which is why individualistic European societies conquered virtually the entire globe with superior technologies and forms of social cooperation.

But the competition for global domination is rarely honest. Thus when Western individualist societies conquered and absorbed collectivist ones, it was only a matter of time before the more intelligent tribes learned how to cheat.

How does one cheat an individualist? By pretending to be an individualist while working as a member of a group. You demand that individualists give you a fair shake in every transaction. But whenever possible, you give preferences to members of your own tribe, and they give preferences to you.

Imagine playing a game of cards in which your opponent can play a wild card but you can't. That wild card is their tribal membership. It does not matter how great an advantage you might have over him in terms of chips at the start, because the rules give him a systematic advantage, and as long as you play the game, you will lose. But individualists are slow to catch on to the scam, *because they are blind to groups.*

It is interesting that the most important founder of modern race- and nation-blind individualism was Ayn Rand, born Alissa Rosenbaum, and the leadership of her Objectivist movement just happened to be overwhelmingly Jewish, including a number of first cousins and married couples. Obviously, this was not individualist meritocracy in action. Yet Rand's followers were blind to this fact as a matter of high moral principle.

There will never be a libertarian society. But libertarian ideology still performs a function within the existing system. And although libertarianism is superficially opposed to the Marxism of the Frankfurt School, both are Jewish intellectual movements that perform the same function: They break down the resistance of high-trust, European individualist societies to duplicitous tribal groups—what John Robb calls "parasite tribes"—preeminently Jews. Libertarians preach individualism, whereas the Frankfurt School stigmatizes white ethnocentrism and extols "inclusiveness" toward "marginalized" groups. But the result is the same. Both doctrines promote Jewish upward mobility and collective power while blinding the rest of society to what is happening.

What kind of people preach blindness as a virtue? People who are up to no good.

Ultimately, I would argue, individualism is a product of the biological and cultural evolution of European man. Individualism goes hand in hand with low ethnocentrism, i.e., openness to strangers, the universalist idea that ultimately there is just one group, humanity, to which we all belong. The European mentality was beautifully encapsulated in a saying of Will Rogers: "A stranger is just a friend you haven't met." I doubt very much that an equivalent phrase can be found in Hebrew or Arabic. In other words, there is fundamentally no us and them. There is just knowledge and ignorance, friends we know and friends we don't.

This openness is highly advantageous because it allows us to increase the number of people with whom trust and cooperation are possible. But openness to strangers is also risky, of course, because they might not reciprocate. Thus taking the risk of sociability—extending the hand of friendship—is deeply engrained in our sense of moral high-mindedness. But when we meet people who do not reciprocate our openness, but instead regard it as a weakness to be exploited, then our virtues are no longer advantageous, and if our elites persist in high-minded openness to such enemies, they must be relieved of their powers and responsibilities.

Individualism blinds its followers to collectivist cheats. Thus the only way to save individualism is to become aware of groups. But that sounds like collectivism. Once we become aware of parasite tribes, we have to exclude them. But that sounds like statism. If individualism is ultimately a European ethos, then individualism requires that we preserve European societies and exclude non-Europeans, which sounds like racial nationalism.

This is the refutation of libertarianism. It is a form of self-refutation. To save individualism, we have to repudiate universalism, reintroduce the distinction between us and them, and start acting collectively. Individualism only works as part of a collective of like-minded people who must exclude collectives that don't play by the same rules. This is how some people start out as libertarian individualists and become racists, anti-Semites, and fascists in the end.

Counter-Currents, October 20, 2015

Why "White" Nationalism?

White Nationalism as I define it is the *right* of all white peoples to sovereign homelands. A *right* is not a *duty*. You are *morally obliged* to do your duty. You merely have the *option* of exercising a right. If, for example, the Swiss Germans are content living in the Swiss Federation, they have no duty to set up their own homeland. But if they feel their identity is threatened by the Swiss Federation and want to exercise their right to secede and form a sovereign homeland, the rest of us have the duty to get out of their way.

Why do I call myself a "White" Nationalist? As an American of European descent, my primary concern is the survival of my race, both on this continent and around the globe. In every white homeland, more whites are dying than being born, and our people are being replaced by highly fertile non-whites. If these trends are not reversed, our race will simply become extinct. The best way to save our race is to create homogeneously white homelands, with pro-natal, pro-eugenic policies. And this means that race must be the basis for defining who belongs to our nations and who does not. Hence White Nationalism.

Now consider the alternatives: *civic nationalism*, which defines the nation legally; *creedal nationalism*, which defines the nation in terms of a common belief system; *linguistic or cultural nationalism*, which defines the nation in terms of a shared language and culture; and *ethnonationalism*, which defines nationality in terms of both common descent and a common culture.

White survival requires the political separation of whites from other races. But civic, creedal, and cultural-linguistic forms of nationalism cannot discriminate between white and non-white, for different races can share legal citizenship, a creed, or a language and culture. Therefore, these forms of nationalism are part of the problem, not part of the solution.

But what about ethnonationalism? How is this an inadequate vehicle for white survival? I think that ethnonationalism *usually is* a good vehicle. Therefore, I *also* call myself an ethnonationalist. Indeed, as I define it, White Nationalism is simply *ethnonationalism for all white peoples*. But there are some important caveats.

First, in the United States and other European colonial societies, old world ethnic identities are increasingly irrelevant as different European stocks blend into new ethnic identities: American, Canadians, etc. Generally, when an American identifies himself as Irish-American or Italian-American, it is simply because he has an Irish or Italian surname. But I know many Italian Americans who are more Irish than Italian, and vice-versa. And even two Americans who have unmixed Irish or Italian ancestry still have more in common with one another in terms of language, culture, and even diet than either of them do with Irishmen or Italians in the Old World.

But the result of this process of blending is not a generic racially white person, but a new ethnic identity: the American. After all, if Americans and Canadians were simply generic white people, there would be no differences between us. But there *are* differences, which are primarily cultural or ethnic, not racial. White Nationalism does mean that *generic white people* have the right to a homeland. It means that *all distinct white peoples* have that right: the French, Germans, and Italians—but also Americans, Canadians, and Quebecois.

Second, colonial societies from the start involved racial distinctions between European colonists and indigenous non-whites. In some cases, African slaves and South and East Asian coolies were added to the mix. In such an environment, it is natural for whites not to see different nations and tribes (Aztec, Mayan), but simply different racial groupings (Indians, blacks, etc.), and it is equally natural for non-whites to see Europeans of different national origins simply as whites. Indeed, in the context of racial polarization and struggle, when whites must present a unified front, the remnants of Old-World ethnic differences are actually harmful to white interests.

Third, within Europe itself, simple ethnic nationalism is not always sufficient to ensure either narrow national or broader racial interests. It is perfectly natural, normal, and right for individuals and nations to take care of their own people first. And when multiethnic empires or multinational bodies like the European Union work against the ethnic interests of specific peoples, then the "petty" nationalism of Scotland or Hungary or Poland is entirely legitimate. However, when petty ethnic nationalism or imperialism lead to wars between European nations, or prevent coordinated European responses to common threats, then a broader sense of pan-European racial solidarity becomes necessary to secure racial survival and flourishing.

Fourth, now that Europe is being colonized by non-whites, the colonial process of racial polarization is taking place there as well. Blacks, Arabs, and South Asians in Europe do not see Frenchmen, Englishmen, and Germans. They simply see white men. And we simply see blacks and browns. Our differences do not matter to them, and their differences do not matter to us. As racial tensions increase in Europe, our people will realize that they are not being attacked as Frenchmen or Germans, but simply as white men. And when Europeans resist ethnic displacement, they will increasingly regard their race as their nation and their skin as their uniform. The sooner we see ourselves as white people, united by common enemies and challenges, sharing a common origin and a common destiny, the sooner we will be equal to the tasks facing us.

Fifth, even though being French or Spanish is about more than simple generic whiteness, being white is still a *necessary condition* of belonging to any European ethnic group, and simply adding that requirement to the naturalization procedures of all European states would have revolutionary positive implications.

But just as I am an ethnonationalist on the condition that it is qualified by a broader white racial solidarity, I am also a White Nationalist on the condition that this preserves rather than undermines distinct white ethnic groups. A broad sense of pan-European solidarity should never become an excuse for the political unification and the cultural and ethnic homogenization of Europe. Thus I fully support the desire of different European peoples to preserve their cultural and biological distinctness. The best vehicle for this is the creation of homogeneous sovereign homelands for all European ethnic groups. The best vehicle for securing pan-European interests is an alliance or federation of sovereign states.

Within colonial societies like the United States, does the emergence of a distinct ethnic identity imply the existence a single white state? Not necessarily. The ethnic unity of white Americans would certainly not stand in the way of such a state. It is perfectly conceivable that the United States might become a homogeneously white society while maintaining its present borders simply by removing its non-white populations.

But White Nationalists should have no absolute commitment to maintaining the present borders of the United States and Canada. Our only absolute goal is white racial preservation. By what means? By any means necessary. Thus if the opportunity arises for states or regions to split off from the United States, perhaps made possible by a collapse of the Federal government or the national economy, White Nationalists should seize upon it.

This is why I have long recommended Harold Covington's Northwest Novels as a stimulus and guide to thinking about how a white homeland might emerge.[1] I don't necessarily think that Covington's particular scenario will play out. Our ability to predict and control events is very limited. Thus, instead of investing a great deal of imagination elaborating a single grand design that probably will never happen, we should explore a whole range of possible scenarios, so that no matter what fate sends our way, we can always turn it to our advantage. Our metapolitical task is not just to make White Nationalism desirable, but to make white homelands conceivable outcomes in a whole array of different circumstances. The only fixed goal is the creation of white homelands. On all other matters, we should be ruthlessly pragmatic.

Counter-Currents, October 30, 2015

---

[1] Greg Johnson, "Birth of a Nation: On Harold Covington's Northwest Quartet," in *In Defense of Prejudice* (San Francisco: Counter-Currents, 2017).

THE SPECTER OF
WHITE NATIONALISM

Greg Hood once pointed out to me that a *White Nationalist Manifesto* could begin with the Preamble of *The Communist Manifesto*, with only a few words changed:

> A specter is haunting the world—the specter of White Nationalism. All the powers that rule over white nations have entered into an unholy alliance to exorcise this specter: church and state, Left and Right, oligarchs and rabble, high culture and low, academia and the lying press.
>
> Where is the party in opposition that has not been decried as "racist" by its opponents in power? Where is the opposition that has not hurled back the searing reproach "they're the *real* racists," against the more advanced opposition parties, as well as against its reactionary adversaries?
>
> Two things result from this fact:
>
> 1. White Nationalism is already acknowledged by all existing powers to be itself a power.
>
> 2. It is high time that White Nationalists should openly, in the face of the whole world, publish their views, their aims, their tendencies, and meet this nursery tale of the Specter of White Nationalism with a manifesto of the movement itself.
>
> To this end, we present the following *Manifesto*.

The parallels are rather uncanny—and rather encouraging, since in a little more than a century, Communism went from being a specter of power to being an actual world power.

The standard game of political parties today is "negative legitimation": They demand your allegiance based not on the positive ground of what they stand for, but simply on the fact that they are *not the other party*. This allows them to avoid standing for any specific platform, and if it gets them into power, they basically have a blank check, so long as they are sufficiently unlike the hated *other party*.

But all of the system's parties quickly unite when any form of white ethnonationalism appears on the scene. White Nationalism is the *other party* for the whole globalist, multicultural, multiracial system. And as the system lurches from crisis to crisis and fails to deliver its promised multicultural paradise, increasingly its only legitimization is *not being us*. The system is so bent on stigmatizing people who stand against multiculturalism and globalization as evil, racist whites, that it will declare George Zimmerman a white man and Donald Trump a Nazi.

But in what sense was Communism a "power" in the 1840s, and in what sense could White Nationalism be a "power" today? In neither case are we speaking about real political power. Instead, White Nationalism today, like Communism back then, is simply an *image of evil*, a bogey man that the system uses to scare the rabble into compliance.

One feels that if we didn't exist, the system would find it necessary to create us. Indeed, in many cases they do create us. First, the system projects images of its diabolical opposites. Of course, these are the diabolical opposites it *prefers*, diabolical opposites that it thinks it can defeat or control. And sometimes rebellious but uncritical minds will adopt these images and act accordingly—so-called "Hollywood Nazis," for example. Second, the system will simply create its own false opposition groups.

Yet for all that, there is a real and growing resistance that is rooted not in the projections and machinations of the system but in the objective reality of racial differences, which make racially and ethnically diverse nations inferior to homogeneous ones. This resistance is growing up through the cracks in the system: the internet, social media, alternative media, and face-to-face groups. Our people are waking up. White Nationalists are now shaping their perceptions and changing their actions. We are showing them the failures of the system, explaining why it is happening, and offering them a workable and inspiring alternative.

But does this make us a power? Being in harmony with reality is certainly an *advantage* in a movement that is largely a debating society. It is also an *advantage* in contending for power with a system premised on lies. Moreover, being in harmony with reality will certainly serve as the *basis* of stable political power, if we can attain it.

But the problem is in the attainment. In itself, truth is not power. The difference between truth and power is the difference between theory and practice, between potentiality and actuality, and a theory we cannot *yet* practice, a potentiality we cannot *yet* actualize, is hardly better than a dream.

How then is a specter of power a real power? It is a power only in the psychological sense. It is the power to incite fear. The establishment uses the specter of White Nationalism to scare the normies. But, increasingly, the establishment itself is afraid of us as well. They think that we are behind Brexit, Trump, Wilders, Le Pen, Alternative for Germany, Orbán, etc. And in a way we are, since we support them, and our ideas also influence them or the people around them.

The establishment has turned White Nationalism into the embodiment of evil, the political equivalent of Satan. This is just the latest version of the ancient slave revolt in morals, in which slaves invert the values of their masters so they can feel good about themselves. Jan Assmann argues that the Jewish ritual law was created by the "normative inversion" of Egyptian religion, and Nietzsche argues that Christian values were created by the normative inversion of Greco-Roman pagan values. Today, every sentiment that preserves distinct peoples from a global homogeneous consumer society—a sense of rootedness and identity, patriotism and love of one's own, a commitment to non-material values, and the willingness to fight and die for them—is labeled evil as well.

This is why evil is so *appealing* in the Judeo-Christian-liberal world: Everything vital, manly, aggressive, lordly, proud, rooted, patriotic, passionate, self-transcending, and glorious is bundled together and labeled evil, whereas everything weak, meek, sniveling, rootless, and self-indulgent is labeled good. All the forces that build civilizations are called evil, whereas everything that dissolves them is deemed good.

The human forebrain can convince itself of such inverted values, particularly individuals with the powerful psychological motive to overthrow the standards by which they are judged inferior. But the values of family and tribe appeal to older parts of the brain, which the forebrain can ignore and repress but never reprogram. Which means that everything we stand for *already appeals to all of our people*—even the most confused and decadent among us—in a deep-seated, literally visceral way.

Everything the system labels *evil* is a psychologically powerful force, not because evil is good, but because biologically healthy values have been defined as evil but remain irresistibly attractive nonetheless. We have power in the imaginations of our people, the power of the dark side. We must take care not to allow the enemy to define us. We have to mock their projections, not own them. But we can exploit the demonic status and emotional power they have granted us and infuse it with our own content. They define everything vital as evil. We can own the vitality and discard their value judgments.

How do we turn psychological power into political power, the specter of White Nationalism into the real thing? We have to make ourselves leaders and get our people to follow us. (The actual history of communism has something to teach us here.) It's a long journey, but it begins with laying the right metapolitical foundations.

An important part of the process is deconstructing the false values that clutter our people's forebrains. We would not have gotten into this position if our conscious moral convictions had no power to determine our behavior.

Equally important, though, is crafting our appeals to the complex of pre-rational sentiments of blood, soil, and honor that our enemies stigmatize and fear. That is not the province of philosophers, but of artists and orators. It is by seizing their passions that we goad our people into action and direct them towards our goals, turning theory into practice and truth into power.

Counter-Currents, April 6, 2017

IS WHITE NATIONALISM UN-AMERICAN?

Many patriotic Americans object to White Nationalism because they are told it is "un-American." America, they say, was always a multiracial society, dedicated to the proposition that "all men are created equal." Therefore, the White Nationalist idea of a society that bases citizenship on race is alien to the American tradition.

This viewpoint is false, based on a systematic misrepresentation of American history.

First of all, the claim that the United States is dedicated to the proposition that "all men are created equal" is simply untrue. The phrase "all men are created equal" comes from the Declaration of Independence of 1776. Whatever the intended meaning of this rhetorical flourish, its author, Thomas Jefferson, and many of the signatories, evidently did not think it was inconsistent with owning Negro slaves. In fact, "all men are created equal" was simply the republican denial of the principle of hereditary monarchy and aristocracy. The intended meaning, however, is moot because the Declaration may well be an important historical document, but it is not a *legal* document of the United States.

The Constitution of the United States was written in 1787, ratified in 1788, and went into effect in 1789. It contains not a word about universal human equality, but it does prohibit a hereditary aristocracy. The Preamble makes it clear that the Constitution was created and ratified by white men to provide good government for themselves and their posterity, not all of mankind. The Constitution treats Indians as foreign nations, allows Negro slavery, and defines free and enslaved blacks as non-citizens, each one counting as only three-fifths of a person for the purposes of Congressional representation.

The claim that America is "dedicated to the proposition" of human equality comes from Abraham Lincoln's Gettysburg Address, which, like the Declaration, is a fine piece of rhetoric, but it is not a legal document of the United States either. Lincoln's claim that America is dedicated to the "proposition" of equality is the epitome of the Left-wing revisionist tradition in America, which has taken a line from the Declaration, inflated it with a great deal of rhetorical hot air, and set it up as the first and final commandment of an egalitarian civil religion. This civil religion has no constitutional basis. But that has proved to be no impediment. A piece of paper still remains enshrined in Washington, D.C. But the Constitution's inegalitarian, particularist, and libertarian order has simply been replaced with a Jacobin-style state committed to realizing the idea of universal human equality.

Second, the claim that America was always a multiracial society—with whites, American Indians, and blacks present from the start of English colonization—is fundamentally false. From the beginning of the colonial period well into the history of the United States, there was a consensus that blacks and American Indians—and later mestizos and Orientals—might be "in" white society, but they were not "of" it. They were foreigners, not fellow citizens. They had no say about the character and destiny of white society.

The colonial consensus that blacks and Indians were not part of white society was reflected in the Constitution. It was further elaborated in the Naturalization Act of 1790, which defined who could become a citizen of the United States. Naturalization was limited to free white persons of good character. This excluded American Indians, indentured servants, free and enslaved blacks, Muslims, and later, Orientals.

From the start, American Indians were considered distinct, sovereign nations. American Indians who did not live on reservations could become citizens only with the adoption of the Fourteenth Amendment in 1868. Citizenship was granted to all American Indians only by the Indian Citizenship Act of 1924. To this day, however, most Indians in effect enjoy dual citizenship, since they belong to tribes which still have special rights granted to them by treaties with the US government.

Blacks, whether slaves or free, were not considered to be part of white society in the colonial period or under the Constitution until the adoption of the 14th Amendment in 1868. The Naturalization Act of 1870 allowed foreign-born blacks, primarily from other parts of the Americas, to become US citizens.

Chinese immigrants began arriving in the 1840s, and their presence almost immediately created a backlash. White Americans objected to Chinese economic competition, drug use, criminality, and all-round alienness.

Soon an Asian exclusion movement arose to cut off Chinese immigration and freeze the Chinese out of American society. The vanguard of Chinese exclusion came from the labor movement, which saw that big business interests were importing coolies to depress white wages and living standards. California was the front line of the Chinese invasion and the white reaction, which was often violent. The Chinese exclusion movement was led by the California Workingmen's Party, founded by Irish immigrant Denis Kearney, who obviously didn't fall for the idea that all immigrants are equal.[1]

---

[1] See Theodore J. O'Keefe's "Denis Kearney and the Struggle for a White America," *Counter-Currents*, February 1, 2001, and Raymond T. Wolters, "Race War on the Pacific Coast," *The Occidental Quarterly*, vol. 8, no. 1 (Spring 2008).

Because of exclusionist agitation, Chinese immigration was reduced, then completely barred for ten years by the Chinese Exclusion Act of 1882, which was renewed in 1892 and again in 1902 and extended to people from Hawaii and the Philippines. Chinese exclusion was again reaffirmed by the Immigration Act of 1924. Chinese born in America were not considered citizens until 1898, and it was only in 1940 that naturalization was opened to people of Chinese, Philippine, and East Indian descent, as well as descendants of the aboriginal peoples from other parts of the Western Hemisphere, meaning Indians and mestizos from outside the United States. Chinese exclusion was only overturned by Congress in 1943, as a wartime gesture toward China.

But even with all of these concessions to non-whites, US immigration and naturalization law was explicitly committed to maintaining an overwhelming white majority until the 1965 Immigration Act threw open America's borders to race-replacement immigration from the Third World.

The 1965 Immigration Act, like the long history of extending citizenship to non-whites that came before it, was imposed by political elites against the will of the white majority. Such measures would never have been approved if the public had been allowed to vote on them in referendums.

Furthermore, extending legal citizenship to non-whites did not in any way alter the deep conviction that real Americans are white, and the naturalization of non-whites came with the expectation that they would live according to white norms. Non-white citizens faced numerous forms of legal and social discrimination, subordination, and segregation well into the 20th century.

Thus, although it is true to say that non-whites have always existed within the borders of what we now call America, throughout most of American history, they have been excluded from citizenship or consigned to second-class citizenship and forced to conform to white cultural norms.

The American tradition of excluding and subordinating non-whites is, of course, portrayed as violent, evil, irrational, petty, and mean-spirited by our education system and culture industry, which are firmly in the hands of the Left. But Americans had their reasons. They recognized that race is real, that the races are different, and that different races are more comfortable in different forms of society. They recognized that any attempt to incorporate non-whites into American society will result in conflict as non-whites demand that white society accommodate them, and whites push back to protect their own way of life. In short, they knew all along precisely what White Nationalists—and white Americans in general—are now learning from bitter experience from the failure of egalitarianism, racial integration, and non-white immigration.

If, dear reader, you truly are an American patriot, if you take your bearings from the American Founding (the real Founding—the Constitution—not the egalitarian afflatus that has replaced it), then it behooves you to learn something about what the founders and subsequent generations of statesmen and sages actually thought about race. I suggest you begin with Jared Taylor's classic article, "What the Founders Really Thought About Race."[2] I also suggest that you pick up S. T. Joshi's *Documents of American Prejudice: An Anthology of Writings on Race from Thomas Jefferson to David Duke*,[3] which documents a long and illus-

---

[2] https://www.scribd.com/document/252361377/What-the-Founders-Really-Thought-About-Race

[3] S. T. Joshi's *Documents of American Prejudice: An Anthology of Writings on Race from Thomas Jefferson to David Duke* (New York: Basic Books, 1999).

trious tradition of American race realism, as well as its editor's Left-wing prejudices.

Even many White Nationalists are surprised to learn how sensible earlier generations of Americans were. This makes America's reversal and decline all the more shocking, but ultimately it is cause for hope, for it reveals deep foundations upon which we can build. Far from being "un-American," White Nationalism is actually the legitimate heir of the healthiest strands of the American tradition.

But unlike previous generations of race realists, who were confused by commitments to classical liberalism, corrupted by the allure of the cheap-labor plantation economy, and too easily contented with half-measures that ultimately failed to preserve America for their posterity, White Nationalists aim at a permanent solution: the repatriation of post-1965 immigrant populations and the partition of the United States into racially homogeneous homelands.

Counter-Currents, April 17, 2017

WHAT IS AMERICAN NATIONALISM?

White Nationalism is not nationalism for undifferentiated, generic white people. Such beings do not exist. Every white person has a specific *ethnic* identity: a mother language and a culture. White Nationalism is ethnic nationalism for all white peoples.

Even in European colonial societies, where different European stocks have blended together, we do not have generic white people. If that were true, there would be no differences between Americans and Canadians. But there are differences, and these differences are ethnic, even though both countries have similar origins, similar histories, similar institutions, and developed on the same continent, right next door to one another. Americans, Canadians, Australians, Quebecois, New Zealanders, etc. are all distinct white ethnic groups.

If Americans are a white ethnicity, then White Nationalists in America should be American nationalists, just as White Nationalists in Hungary are Hungarian nationalists, White Nationalists in Poland are Polish Nationalists, White Nationalists in Quebec are Quebecois nationalists, and so forth.

What is the message of White Nationalists who take up the banner of true American nationalism? Basically, it is the same message as White Nationalists everywhere: Race is real, ethnicity is real, and racial and ethnic diversity within the same country is not a strength but a weakness: a source of alienation, friction, inefficiency, cultural debasement, long-simmering resentments, and even hatred and violence. Therefore, the best way to ensure peace between different ethnic groups, as well as to afford them maximum latitude for independent development, is to create sovereign homelands for all peoples who desire to control their own destinies. Since Americans are a distinct white ethnicity, American nationalism means turning America into a homogeneously white homeland.

The inevitable objection to American Nationalism is that America is not a white society with a common culture but a multiracial, multicultural society unified not by common blood, or by a common culture, but by a commitment to a civic creed—a central principle of which is the proposition that "All men are created equal"—as well as the "American dream" of ever-rising material standards of living. This is the "civic" as opposed to "racial/ethnic" version of American nationalism.

Interestingly enough, this objection does not come from the far Left, which maintains that even today America is a "normatively white" and "white supremacist" society, regardless of the presence of other races on our soil. Instead, the civic interpretation of American nationalism is asserted primarily by people on the center-Left and the center-Right. But recently they have been joined by White Nationalists and Southern Nationalists, who argue that White Nationalists cannot be American nationalists, because American nationalism is somehow intrinsically and essentially civic nationalist.

There is no question that most Americans today believe in the civic nationalist conception of American identity. But they've simply been fooled. As I have argued in my essay, "Is White Nationalism Un-American?," American civic nationalism is a fundamentally false interpretation of American history and identity that has been imposed upon the American mind by comprehensive propaganda in education and the mass media.

America was not founded as a society "dedicated to the proposition" that "all men are created equal." The phrase "all men are created equal" is found in the Declaration of Independence, which is not a legal document of the Unit-

ed States. The phrase is simply a denial of hereditary king-
ship and aristocracy, not a blanket claim that all men—
and especially all races—are equal.

The Preamble to the US Constitution specifies its aims:

> We the People of the United States, in Order to
> form a more perfect Union, establish Justice, insure
> domestic Tranquility, provide for the common de-
> fence, promote the general Welfare, and secure the
> Blessings of Liberty to ourselves and our Posterity,
> do ordain and establish this Constitution for the
> United States of America.

Note that there is nothing about promoting the "proposition" that all men are created equal, or any propositions
at all for that matter. Instead, the purpose of the US government is to promote concrete social goods: justice, do-
mestic and international security, the common good, and
liberty.

Moreover, the Constitution only promotes its aims for
the founders and their posterity, not all of mankind. And
it went without saying that the founders and their posterity were white people.

The claim that the United States was founded in 1776
to promote universal human equality comes from Lincoln's Gettysburg Address, another piece of high-minded
rhetorical flummery which is not a legal document of the
United States either.

Although the Constitution does not spell out the race
of the founders and their "posterity," the Naturalization
Act of 1790—which deals with people who were not born
American, i.e., people who were not the posterity of the
founders—made very clear that the only people who
could join the American polity as citizens were free white
people of good character (i.e., excluding convicts and indentured servants).

The United States did not allow blacks to become citizens until 1868. Blacks from other parts of the Americas could become citizens only after 1870. American Indians who did not live on reservations could become citizens in 1868. Citizenship was granted to all American Indians only by the Indian Citizenship Act of 1924. Chinese immigration began in the 1840s but was banned from 1882 to 1943, and Chinese born in America were not considered citizens until 1898. Only in 1940 was naturalization opened to people of Chinese, Philippine, and East Indian descent, as well as Indians and mestizos from other parts of the Americas. But each extension of citizenship to non-whites was fiercely resisted. Moreover, until 1965, American immigration laws were designed to maintain a white supermajority with an ethnic balance based on the 1890 census.

But even after America's white supremacist immigration laws were scrapped in 1965, America still remained a *culturally* and *normatively* white society. For people around the world, an American simply means a white person. Hence the necessity of phrases like African-American and Asian-American. This is why I have always opposed white Americans calling themselves "European-Americans," because the phrase is as redundant as "feline lion" or "canine mastiff." Beyond that, calling ourselves European-Americans implicitly abandons the normative whiteness of American identity and puts us on the same level as non-whites, who are Americans only in a legal sense of the word.

When America's white founders created the Constitution to bequeath good government to their white posterity—and when they specified that the only foreigners who could become American citizens were free white people of good character—they were declaring that a free and orderly white society is every American's birthright.

But this birthright was stolen from us. Three principal forces were responsible for the undoing of white America:

❖ The cheap labor/plantation model of capitalism, which imported black slaves, Chinese
coolies, and mestizo stoop labor to undercut
the wages of free white workers
❖ Christian and liberal universalism and egalitarianism, which regard natural partialities to
family and nation as illegitimate
❖ Jewish ethnic lobbying to create a conception
of America that was maximally open to Jewish
immigration and upward mobility

The goal of American White Nationalism is to restore
the free white nation that is our birthright.

American White Nationalism is far more likely to win
the battle for a white homeland than anti-American forms
of White Nationalism. The white Americans who lean toward white identity politics, even implicitly, overwhelmingly vote for the Republican Party. They also tend to be
conservative and patriotic. They identify with America
and feel a strong attachment to American symbols.

Like everyone else in our society, they have been mis-
educated about America's nature and history and think it
was founded as a color-blind propositional nation.

But they are also increasingly aware of the catastrophic
consequences of diversity. Thus as white demographic
displacement accelerates, these Americans will become
increasingly receptive to our account of America's real
identity, how our country has been hijacked by hostile
aliens, and how we can Make America White Again.

By contrast, anti-American White Nationalists will
have to convince our people of all the same facts about
race, diversity, and demographic displacement. But, as if
that were not already enough of an uphill battle, they will
also have to sell Americans a raft of anti-American ideas:
Southern Nationalism, cranky conspiracy theories about
Freemasons, and the like. The anti-Americans will also

have to convince Americans of a whole host of historical revisionist theses about the Civil War, the Third Reich, and the holocaust, none of them really necessary for white survival in America. Finally, the anti-Americans will have to explain away their use of symbols which are at best alien to Americans and at worst are freighted with highly negative connotations.

Both forms of White Nationalism communicate the same truths. But American nationalists relate them to ideas that feel authentic to our target audience, while anti-American nationalists link them to ideas that at best strike most Americans as alien and inauthentic and at worse seem downright repugnant.

Which approach is likely to make more converts? Which approach is more likely to save the white race in America, which is really the only thing that matters?

I believe that anti-American White Nationalism is self-marginalizing and self-defeating. American nationalism is the only way forward.

True American nationalism is a form of White Nationalism, and true White Nationalism in America is American nationalism.

Counter-Currents, March 20, 2018

IS WHITE NATIONALISM
HATEFUL?

One of the most common charges against White Nationalism is that it is an ideology of hatred toward other groups. My answer is: "Yes, but so what?" Yes, because hatred of other groups is definitely one factor in White Nationalism. So what, because hate does not disqualify White Nationalism, for two reasons: (1) ethnic hatred is a universal phenomenon in racially and culturally diverse societies, and (2) unlike the proponents of multiculturalism, White Nationalists actually offer a realistic path to reducing ethnic hatred and violence by reducing racial and cultural diversity. Beyond that, multiculturalists are hypocrites for denouncing hatred in our hearts while harboring it in theirs.

Sometimes, our accusers will spice up the hate charge by saying that we hate non-whites "just because they are different"—as if the norm for human relations is to *like* people who are different, thus disliking people who are different is morally depraved. Now, of course, we often do like people *in spite of the fact* that they are different. But that is not good enough for multiculturalists. For if diversity is self-evidently and unconditionally good, then we should like other people not in spite of their differences, but *because* of them.

So is it normal for human beings to like or dislike people because of their differences? Do birds of a feather flock together? Or do opposites attract? Common sense, history, and science (specifically Genetic Similarity Theory) all support the idea that genetic similarity and a common culture promote harmony between individuals. Ethnocentrism is the preference for the genetically similar over the genetically different. Ethnocentrism is wired into the human brain, an inheritance of our prehuman evolutionary history in which even creatures as simple as ants and bees have the ability to distinguish between degrees of relatedness and show marked preference for their own kin. The greater the genetic and cultural differences between people, the greater the tension and conflict. Thus when people from different races and cultures are forced to live together in the same society, the predictable result is not a rainbow of tolerance, but constant friction, simmering hatred, and even outbursts of violence.

Some White Nationalists wish to deny that hatred plays any part in our politics. But if we believe that racial and cultural diversity in the same country cause hatred, then we are of course not immune to those forces. Indeed, if we were exposed to diversity and did not end up hating other groups, that would amount to a refutation of our own argument for White Nationalism. Thus it is self-defeating to protest that we don't actually hate members of other groups.

I will grant that ethnic hated is not *necessarily* a part of White Nationalism, since people can arrive at our positions based simply on science, history, and common sense, without necessarily having any negative experiences of other groups. But of course people can also develop ethnic hatreds without personal experience of other groups.

I will also grant that it is possible to like individual members of racial and ethnic groups that one dislikes as a whole. Traits are distributed on bell curves, after all, and there will always be likable outliers even in enemy groups. The problem is that there are just not enough good blacks, good Jews, good mestizos, or good Muslims for us to get along in a diverse society.

I will further grant that love of our own group is more fundamental than hatred of outgroups. But that still does not imply that we do not feel hatred toward other groups when exposed to diversity. Hatred of our enemies and rivals is just the flip side of loving our own. And the stronger the love, the stronger the hatreds as well.

White Nationalists, then, are not immune to the problems of diversity. But neither is anyone else in a multicultural society. The only differences between White Nationalists and the rest of our people are (1) we are more attuned to racial and ethnic differences, (2) we thus become aware of the problems of diversity sooner than others, and (3) we are more honest about our feelings. But the rest of our people have the same nature and the same reactions to outgroups. Thus they will eventually come to feel the same way. And this is true even of the advocates of multiculturalism.

Hatred of other groups is the norm in racially and culturally diverse societies. But, as I put it in the title essay of my first book, *Confessions of a Reluctant Hater*, White Nationalists don't want to hate other groups. The whole point of White Nationalism is to offer a real solution to ethnic hatred and violence: reducing diversity by creating racially and culturally homogeneous homelands. Multiculturalists, by contrast, wish to increase racial and cultural diversity, which will only lead to increased hatred and violence between groups.

The charge of hatred is so stigmatizing because most people think that hatred is intrinsically evil and love is intrinsically good. Our heads echo with a thousand silly pop songs extolling love as the answer, and childish movie dialogue like Obi-Wan Kenobi intoning, "Luke! Don't give in to hate. That leads to the Dark Side."

But love is not always a good thing. If you enable an evil person out of love, then love is a bad thing. And hate is not always a bad thing. Hatred toward evil people is perfectly reasonable, just, and good, and can lead to a better world. Thus the proper answer to the charge of being a hater is, "Yes, but is it the good kind of hate or the bad kind?" And when someone oh-so-bravely declares that he is on the side of "love," one should answer, "Sure, but is it the good kind of love or the bad kind?"

If you think that hate is always evil and love is always good, then naturally you will want to *command* people to feel love and not to feel hate. It is simply what they *ought* to do. But emotions cannot be commanded this way. Emotions like love and hate are evolved responses to objective facts. Trying to command them is like trying to command your pupils not to dilate when you walk into a darkened room.

Thus if you believe that you are morally obligated to love rather than hate, this will not actually change your feelings. It will simply give you an incentive to lie about them to yourself and others. The moral imperative to love diversity has no power to change the wiring of our brains, which love similarity, not diversity. The only power the multicultural imperative has is to make liars and hypocrites of us all. The only way to actually reduce hatred of racially and culturally different people is to reduce diversity by giving people their own homogeneous homelands.

When multiculturalists condemn us as haters, the proper response is to knock them off their high horse by pointing out their obvious hypocrisy. Everybody hates somebody. Multiculturalists obviously hate white people. They say that they hate whites, and they teach the most impressionable whites to hate themselves. They especially hate White Nationalists.

So there's plenty of hate to go around here. The real issues are whether our hatred is *reasonable* or not, whether we are *honest* about our feelings or not, and whether we have *realistic proposals* to change the realities that make ethnic hatred and violence inevitable. For White Nationalists, the answer is yes in all three cases.

Multiculturalists, however, hate us because we reject the false values and unworkable model of society to which they are wedded. That is unreasonable. Multiculturalists have ethnocentric feelings too, but they lie about them and often avoid the diversity that they wish to foist on the rest of us. That is dishonest and hypocritical. Finally, multiculturalists decry ethnic hatred and violence but continue to promote the diversity that makes these problems inevitable. Such irresponsibility should disqualify them from holding any positions of political power and influence.

Thus White Nationalists have good reason to hate multiculturalists for their morally squalid characters and for the evils they have unleashed on white nations. Indeed, it is more appropriate for us to hate the white multiculturalists who have created this situation than the non-whites who are merely taking advantage of it. Traitors are worse than enemies. Frankly, if they had a shred of decency, multiculturalists would hate themselves a bit as well.

Counter-Currents, April 3, 2017

WHY BOOMERS NEED NOT FEAR WHITE NATIONALISM

I don't like anti-Boomer memes. We need to convert as many of our people as possible, not write off vast swathes of the white population. And pitting one generation against another strikes me as a Jewish tactic of culture warfare, as we saw when the Boomers were incited to revolt against their parents' generation.

But there is an argument that Boomers use against us that we can turn to our advantage.

The post-war Baby Boom generation encompasses everyone born in America between 1946 and 1964. In 2018, the oldest Boomers are turning 72. The youngest are turning 54.

Whites are projected to become a numerical minority in America around 2050, give or take a few years. In 2050, the oldest Boomers will be 104; the youngest will be 86. Which means that most of them will be dead by the time we become a minority. So many Boomers think that white demographic decline is simply not their problem.

Of course this is a terrible argument for not doing something to prevent an oncoming catastrophe—and the fate of whites in South Africa is a foretaste of what our people can expect when they become a hated minority in this country. The world does not end when we die. We have obligations to future generations—such as not visiting hell-on-earth upon them.

"I'll be dead then, so it is not my problem" is a completely egocentric, self-indulgent, and irresponsible outlook—but it is the dominant ethos of our culture today—at least when white interests are discussed. Very different standards come into play when we consider the interests of non-whites, the extinction of animal species, and long-term environmental trends. Suddenly, the long view and expansive duties to others, even future generations, become the norm.

The Boomers are the first generation to make widespread use of abortion and birth control, killing or simply refusing to conceive the next generation merely to maximize their pleasure in the present day. But later generations are not ones to talk. Our whole culture is afflicted with selfish hedonism that is aborting the future of our race. It is hard to ask such people to care about future generations.

In the case of the Boomers, however, this selfishness can work in our favor. Boomers don't fear white demographic decline, because it will happen after they are dead. But by the same token, Boomers should not fear White Nationalism either, for the creation of a white ethnostate will only happen after their deaths as well. As outlined in my essay "Restoring White Homelands,"[1] the process of creating a white ethnostate in an orderly and humane fashion would take decades.

As I envision it, White Nationalism would be established in three phases. First, if White Nationalists came to power tomorrow, we could immediately restore the idea of America as a *normatively* white society. That would simply be a matter of will. Second, we could change our immigration/emigration policies to aim at gradually restoring the ethnic *status quo* of 1965 by 2065. We would also remove all forms of forced racial integration. This would yield 90%-White Nationalism nationwide, and *de facto* White Nationalism for any white person who wanted it. Third, in 2065, we could then begin to establish racially homogeneous ethnostates.

But in 2065, the youngest Boomers will be turning 101. So Boomers have nothing to fear from White National-

---

[1] In *The White Nationalist Manifesto*.

ism. They will never live to see it. It isn't their problem.

But even if Boomers will all be dead by the time we create Whitopia, wouldn't it be reasonable for them to fear present-day manifestations of White Nationalism, people like Dylann Roof and James Fields? Honestly, no. Boomers don't fear or oppose present-day manifestations of white demographic decline—including enormous increases in crime committed by non-whites—as long as they don't affect them personally. So as long as we can convince Boomers that the Dylann Roofs and James Fields of the world are *other people's problems*, not theirs, they won't be worried. Boomers are far more likely to be killed by Muslim terrorists than White Nationalists, and if Boomers don't care about the greater problem, why would they care about a lesser one? Of course if I had my way, there would be no more spree killers or Unite the Rights. But as far as Boomers are concerned, as long as bodies don't show up on the golf course, they won't be troubled.

So our message to the Boomers is: Go ahead and spend your kids' inheritances. You'll never live to see the grim, burrito-free dystopia we are creating, where alienation is replaced with kinship and community; where you can read the signs, understand the words, and trust the intentions of the people around you; where, after long lives of mowing their own damn lawns, old people will die surrounded by generations of their posterity, rather than in nursing homes surrounded by thieving and abusive brown people. If white demographic decline is not your problem, because you'll be dead before things become unbearable, then neither is the inevitable reaction, which is White Nationalism.

TECHNOLOGICAL UTOPIANISM & ETHNIC NATIONALISM

This is the text of my talk at the fourth meeting of the Scandza Forum in Copenhagen, Denmark, on September 15, 2018. In my previous Scandza Forum talk, "Redefining the Mainstream" (reprinted below), I argued that we need to craft ethnonationalist messages for all white groups, even Trekkies. This is my Epistle to the Trekkies.

The idea of creating a utopian society through scientific and technological progress goes back to such founders of modern philosophy as Bacon and Descartes, although the idea was already hinted at by Machiavelli. But today, most people's visions of technological utopia are derived from science fiction. With the notable exception of Frank Herbert's *Dune* series,[1] science fiction tends to identify progress with political liberalism and globalism. Just think of *Star Trek*, in which the liberal, multi-racial Federation is constantly battling against perennial evils like nationalism and eugenics. Thus it is worth asking: Is ethnic nationalism—which is illiberal and anti-globalist—compatible with technological utopianism or not?

My view is that technological utopianism is not only *compatible* with ethnic nationalism but also that *liberalism and globalization undermine technological progress*, and that *the ethnostate is actually the ideal incubator for mankind's technological apotheosis*.

Before arguing these points, however, I need to say a bit about what technological utopianism entails and why

---

[1] Greg Johnson, "Archaeofuturist Fiction: Frank Herbert's *Dune*," *Counter-Currents*, August 15, 2014.

people think it is a natural fit with globalization. The word *utopia* literally means *nowhere* and designates a society that cannot be realized. But the progress of science and technology are all about *the conquest of nature,* i.e., the expansion of man's power and reach, so that utopia becomes attainable. Specific ambitions of scientific utopianism include the abolition of material scarcity, the exploration and settlement of the galaxy, the prolongation of human life, and the upward evolution of the human species.

It is natural to think that scientific and technological progress go hand-in-hand with globalization. Reality is one, therefore the science that understands reality and the technology that manipulates it must be one as well. Science and technology speak a universal language. They are cumulative collaborative enterprises that can mobilize the contributions of the best people from across the globe. So it seems reasonable that the road to technological utopia can only be impeded by national borders. I shall offer three arguments why this is not so.

1. GLOBALIZATION VS. INNOVATION

I define globalization as breaking down barriers to sameness: the same market, the same culture, the same form of government, the same way of life—what Alexandre Kojève called the "universal homogeneous state."

As Peter Thiel argues persuasively in *Zero to One,* globalization and technological innovation are actually two very different modes of progress.[2] Technological innovation creates something new. Globalization merely copies new things and spreads them around. Thiel argues, furthermore, that globalization without technological innovation is not sustainable. For instance, it is

---

[2] Peter Thiel, *Zero to One: Notes on Startups, or How to Build the Future* (New York: Crown, 2014).

simply not possible for China and India to consume as much fossil fuel as the First World countries, but that is entailed by globalization within the present technological context. In the short run, this sort of globalization will have catastrophic environmental effects. In the long run, it will hasten the day when our present form of civilization collapses when fossil fuels are exhausted. To stave off this apocalypse, we need new innovations, particularly in the area of energy.

The most important technological innovations of the 20th century are arguably splitting the atom and the conquest of space. Neither was accomplished by private enterprise spurred by consumer demand in a global liberal-democratic society. Instead, they were created by rival governments locked in hot and cold warfare: first the United States and its Allies against the Axis powers in World War II, then the United States and the capitalist West versus the Soviet Bloc until the collapse of Communism in 1989–1991.

Indeed, one can argue that the rivalry between capitalism and communism began to lose its technological dynamism because of the statesmanship of Richard Nixon, who began détente with the USSR with the Strategic Arms Limitations Talks in 1969, then went to China in 1971, lessening the threat that the Communist powers would recoalesce into a single bloc. Détente ended with the Soviet invasion of Afghanistan in 1979. Ronald Reagan's Strategic Defense Initiative could have spurred major technological advances, but merely threatening it was enough to persuade Gorbachev to seek a political solution. So the ideal situation for spurring technological growth is *political rivalry without political resolution*, thereby necessitating immense expenditures on research and development to gain technological advantages.

Since the collapse of Communism and the rise of a unipolar liberal-democratic world order, however, the driving force of technological change has been consumer demand. Atomic energy and sending men into space have been pretty much abandoned, and technological progress has been primarily channeled into information technology, which has made some of us more productive but for the most part just allows us to amuse ourselves with smartphones as society declines around us.

But we are not going to be able to Tweet ourselves out of looming environmental crises and Malthusian traps. Only fundamental innovations in energy technology will do the trick. And only the state, which can command enormous resources and unite a society around a common purpose, has a record of accomplishment in this area.

Of course none of the parties to the great conflicts that spurred technological growth were ethnonationalists in the strict sense, not even the Axis powers. Indeed, liberal democracy and communism were merely rival visions of global society. But when rival visions of globalization are slugging it out for power, that means that the globe is divided among a plurality of different political actors.

Pluralism and rivalry have spurred states to the greatest technological advances in history. Globalization, pacification, and liberalism have not only halted progress but have bred complacency in the face of potential global disasters. A global marketplace will never take mankind to the stars. It will simply distract us until civilization collapses and the Earth becomes a scorched boneyard.

2. INNOVATION VS. COST-CUTTING

In economics, productivity is defined as a mathematical formula: outputs divided by inputs, i.e., the cost per widget. Mathematically speaking, you can increase productivity either by making labor more productive, chiefly through technological innovation, or simply by cutting costs.

Most of the productivity gains that come from economic globalization are a matter of cost-cutting, primarily cutting the costs of labor. The Third World has a vast supply of cheap labor. Economic globalization allows the free movement of labor and capital. Businesses can cut labor costs by moving factories overseas or by importing new workers to drive down wages at home.

Historically speaking, the greatest economic spur to technological innovation has been high labor costs. The way to raise labor costs is to end economic globalization,[3] by cutting off immigration and by putting high tariffs on foreign manufactured goods. In short, we need economic nationalism. Indeed, only economic nationalism can lead to a post-scarcity economy.

What exactly is a "post-scarcity economy," and how can we get there from here? First of all, not all forms of scarcity can be abolished. Unique and handcrafted items will always be scarce. There will only be one *Mona Lisa*. Scarcity can only be abolished with identical, mass-produced items. Second, the cost of these items will only approach zero in terms of labor. Basically, we will arrive at a post-scarcity economy when machines put everyone involved in mass production out of work. But the machines, raw materials, and energy used in production will still have some costs. Thus the post-scarcity economy will arrive through innovation in robotics and energy production. The best image of a post-scarcity world is the "replicator" in *Star Trek*, which can change the atomic structure of basic inputs to materialize things out of thin air.

Of course workers who are replaced by machines can't be allowed to starve. The products of machines have to

---

[3] Greg Johnson, "The End of Globalization," in *Truth, Justice, & a Nice White Country*.

be consumed by someone. Production can be automated but consumption cannot. It would be an absurdist dystopia if mechanization led to the starvation of workers, so consumption had to be automated as well. One set of robots would produce things, then another set of robots would consume them and add zeroes to the bank balances of a few lonely plutocrats.

To make the post-scarcity economy work, we need to ensure that people can afford to buy its products. There are two basic ways this can be done.

First, the productivity gains of capital have to be shared with the workers, through rising wages or shrinking work weeks. When workers are eliminated entirely, they need to receive generous pensions.

Second, every economic system requires a medium of exchange. Under the present system, the state gives private banks the ability to create money and charge interest on its use. The state also provides a whole range of direct payments to individuals: welfare, old-age pensions, etc. A *universal basic income* is a direct government payment to *all* citizens that is sufficient to ensure basic survival in a First World country.[4] Such an income would allow the state to ensure economic liquidity, so that every product has a buyer, while eliminating two very costly middlemen: banks and social welfare bureaucracies.

All of this sounds pretty far out. But it is only unattainable in the present globalized system, in which cost-cutting is turning high-tech, First World industrial economies into low-tech Third World cheap-labor plantation economies. Only economic nationalism can spur the technological innovations necessary to create a post-scarcity economy by raising labor costs, both through

---

[4] Greg Johnson, "Money for Nothing," in *Truth, Justice, & a Nice White Country.*

immigration controls and tariff walls against cheap foreign manufactured goods.

3. ETHNONATIONALISM & SCIENCE

So far we have established that scientific and technological progress are undermined by globalization and
encouraged by nationalist economic policies and the rivalries between nations and civilizational blocs. But we
need a more specific argument to establish that ethnonationalism is especially in harmony with scientific and
technological progress.

My first premise is: *No form of government is fully
compatible with scientific and technological progress if it
is founded on dogmas that are contrary to fact.* For instance, the republic of Oceania might have a population
of intelligent and industrious people, an excellent educational system, first rate infrastructure, and a booming
economy. But if the state religion of Oceania mandates
that the Earth is flat and lies at the center of the uni-
verse, Oceania is not going to take us to the stars.

My second premise is: *The advocacy of racially and
ethnically diverse societies—regardless of whether they
have liberal or conservative regimes—is premised on the
denial of political experience and the science of human
biological diversity.*

The history of human societies offers abundant evi-
dence that putting multiple ethnic groups under the
same political system is a recipe for otherwise avoidable
ethnic tensions and conflicts. Furthermore, science indicates that the most important factors for scientific and
technological advancement—intelligence and creativity—are primarily genetic, and they are not equally distributed among the races. Finally, Genetic Similarity
Theory predicts that the most harmonious and happy
societies will be the most genetically homogeneous, with
social conflict increasing with genetic diversity.

Denying these facts is anti-scientific in two ways. First and most obviously, it is simply the refusal to look at objective facts that contradict the dogma that diversity improves society. Second, basing a society on this dogma undermines the genetic and social conditions necessary for progress and innovation, for instance by lowering the average IQ and creating greater social conflict. Other things being equal, these factors will make a society less likely to foster scientific and technological innovation.

My third premise is: *Ethnonationalism is based on both political experience and the science of human biological diversity—and does not deny any other facts.* Therefore, *ethnonationalism is more compatible with scientific and technological progress than are racially and ethnically diverse societies—other things being equal.*

Of course some research and development projects require so much money and expertise that they can only be undertaken by large countries like the United States, China, India, or Russia. Although we can predict with confidence that all of these societies would improve their research and development records if they were more racially and culturally homogeneous, even in their present states they can accomplish things that small, homogeneous ethnostates simply cannot dream of.

For instance, if a country of two million people like Slovenia were to adopt ethnonationalism, it would probably outperform a more diverse society with the same size and resources in research and development. But it would not be able to colonize Mars. However, just as small countries can defend themselves from big countries by creating alliances, small states can work together on scientific and technological projects too big to undertake on their own. But no alliance is stronger than its weakest member. Since diversity is a weakness and homogeneity is a strength, we can predict that cooperative research and development efforts among ethnostates will probably be more fruitful than those among diverse societies.

Now someone might object that one can improve upon the ethnostate by taking in only high-IQ immigrants from other races. Somehow Americans went to the Moon without importing Asians and Indians. Such people are being imported today for two reasons. First, importing foreign brains allows us to evade problems with producing our own, namely, dysgenic fertility and the collapse of American STEM education, largely due to political correctness, i.e., racial integration and the denial of biological intelligence differences. Second, the productivity gains attributed to diversity in technology are simply due to cost-cutting. But the real answer is: The internet allows whites to collaborate with the best scientists around the world. So we don't need to live with them.

To sum up: The idea that technological utopia will go hand-in-hand with the emergence of a global homogeneous society is false. The greatest advances in technology were spurred by the rivalries of hostile political powers, and with the emergence of a unipolar world, technological development has been flagging.

The idea that technological utopia goes hand-in-hand with liberal democracy is false. Liberalism from its very inception has been opposed to the idea that there is a common good of society. Liberalism is all about empowering individuals to pursue private aims and advantages. It denies that the common good exists; or, if the common good exists, liberalism denies that it is knowable; or if the common good exists and is knowable, liberalism denies that it can be pursued by the state, but instead will be brought about by an invisible hand if we just allow private individuals to go about their business.

The only thing that can bring liberal democrats together to pursue great common aims is the threat of war. This is what sent Americans to the Moon. America's greatest technological achievements were fostered by the government, not private enterprise, and in times of hot and cold war, not peace. Since the end of the Cold War, however, victory has defeated us. America is no longer a serious country.

The solution, though, is not to go back to war, but to junk liberalism and return to the classical idea that there is a common good that can and must be pursued by the state. A liberal democracy can only be a serious country if someone like the Russians threatens to nuke them every minute of the day. Normal men and normal societies pursue the common good, because once one is convinced something really is good, one needs no additional reason to pursue it. But if you need some extra incentives, consider the environmental devastation and civilizational collapse that await us as the fossil fuel economy continues to expand like an algae bloom to its global limits. That should concentrate the mind wonderfully.

The idea that technological utopia will go hand-in-hand with global capitalism is false. Globalization has undermined technological innovation by allowing businesses to raise profits merely by cutting costs. The greatest advances in manufacturing technology have been spurred by high labor costs, which are products of a strong labor movement, closed borders, and protectionism.

Finally, the idea that technological utopianism will go hand-in-hand with racially and ethnically diverse societies is false. This is where ethnonationalism proves its superiority. Diversity promotes social conflict and removes barriers to dysgenic breeding. The global average IQ is too low to create a technological utopia. Global race-mixing will make Europeans more like the global average. Therefore, it will extinguish all dreams of progress. Ethnonationalists, however, are actually willing to replace dysgenic reproductive trends with eugenic ones, to ensure that every future generation has more geniuses, including scientific ones. And if you need an extra incentive, consider the fact that China is pursuing eugenics while in the West it is fashionable to adopt Haitian babies. Ethnonationalism, moreover, promotes social harmony and cohesion, which make possible coordinated efforts toward common goals.

What sort of society will conquer scarcity, conquer death, and settle the cosmos? A society that practices economic nationalism to encourage automation. A homogeneous, high-IQ society with eugenic rather than dysgenic reproductive trends. A harmonious, cohesive, high-trust society that can work together on common projects. An illiberal society that is willing to mobilize its people and resources to achieve great common aims. In short, if liberal democracy and global capitalism are returning us to the mud, it is ethnonationalism that will take us to the stars.

Counter-Currents, September 17, 2018

FREEDOM OF SPEECH

*This is my speech at the third Erkenbrand Confer-
ence in the Netherlands on Saturday, November 3,
2018.*

I've got good news and bad news.

The good news is that everyone likes to get good
news. It is easy to bring good news and easy to receive it.

The bad news is that nobody likes to get bad news. It
is hard to bring bad news and hard to receive it. Receiving bad news is upsetting, which is why bringing bad
news is difficult. Sometimes one has to deal with tears
and anger.

But bad news is always more important than good
news, because if something is going wrong you need to
know. Bad news is not a problem. Bad news is one's
awareness of a problem. And no matter how bad a problem is, it is usually better to know than not know, because knowing about a problem is the first step towards
fixing it. The only situation in which it might be better
not to know is if a problem is insoluble, so that knowing
about it simply adds to the problem rather than helps
alleviate it.

Because bad news is upsetting, people often respond
to it irrationally. Sometimes they would prefer not to
know, even though you can't solve problems you don't
know about. Sometimes they misplace their emotions.
Instead of getting upset with the problem itself and seek-
ing to solve it, they get upset with the bad news and seek
to punish the bearer. But this is foolish, because society
works best when information flows freely, and the most
important information is bad news.

Because receiving bad news is upsetting and giving it

is risky, dealing with bad news is a test of character. Those who receive bad news have to master their emotions, for if you dissolve into tears or explode into anger, you are making it more burdensome to bring you bad news in the future, which means that you might not receive news about a problem until it is too late to rectify it. Bringing bad news is also a test of character, because one always risks unpleasant personal consequences, but sometimes short-run personal risks are necessary to secure the greater good in the long run. But since the bearers of bad news are doing us all a favor, it is incumbent upon us to reduce the risks to the absolute minimum. This is why freedom of speech needs to be a right enshrined in the fundamental law of every land.

One does not need the right to freedom of speech to tell people what they want to hear. Freedom of speech is the freedom to tell people what they don't want to hear—but need to hear anyway. A right to freedom of speech, moreover, is not necessary when one bears bad news to powerless people, for instance one's children, one's students, or one's employees. After all, they can't punish you for your good deed. We need the *right* to freedom of speech when we bear bad news to people who are more powerful than us—people who need bad news to make important decisions, and people who have the power to punish the bearers of bad news. But they can't punish us if free speech is our right. Our rights trump their anger.

The two most important things for White Nationalists today are:

First, breaking down the taboo against white identity politics, i.e., the idea that it is *immoral* for whites—and only whites—to take our own side in ethnic conflicts.

Second, maintaining our freedom of speech long enough to destroy that taboo.

White Nationalists are the bearers of bad news: that

diversity is not a strength, but a source of alienation, conflict, and violence; that modern politics and morals have put our race on a path to extinction; and the only solution is to abandon liberalism, hedonistic individualism, globalization, and multiculturalism and bring back healthier, pro-white policies and values. We are changing people's minds, and the establishment is powerless to change them back. Thus they are trying to censor us.

How can we deal with this threat?

In the short run, we need an internet Bill of Rights to protect dissidents from censorship and deplatforming. Beyond that, we need an across-the-board ban on politically-correct terms of service and employment, so we are free to dissent without threatening our livelihoods and social capital. If we can get such legislation in place, I am confident that we can win, and sooner rather than later. We will change so many minds that we will reach a tipping point. The taboo against white identity politics will melt away. Pro-white values will pervade the culture. Eventually we can mobilize enough support to overthrow the existing political establishment and replace it with a pro-white one.

But who told us that this would be safe and easy? White Nationalists are battling against the most all-encompassing soft-totalitarian system in history. It is a system bent on nothing short of the genocide of the white race, a goal so evil that when Plato and Aristotle drew up their lists of bad regimes, it was simply inconceivable. To overthrow this system, we might have to risk much more than our livelihoods. We might have to risk our very lives.

In the long run, though, we are probably going to win even if we don't get an internet Bill of Rights. Censorship can slow us down, but it can't really stop us. Already people are laying the foundations for a new internet that will be free of the choke points where censors perch.

Thus, ultimately, the only way to prevent us from getting our message out online will be to shut down the web entirely. But the establishment cannot contemplate that, because the global political and economic system depends on the internet.

The establishment—or at least the tiny stratum that is fully aware of the present threat of white identity politics—has the same relationship to the internet as a junkie to his habit. He knows that it will kill him in the long run. But very few junkies overcome their addiction because they cannot bear the short-term pain, even if it is the price of long-term survival.

Human beings might best be defined as the intermittently rational animal, and one of the most pervasive forms of irrationality is pursuing short-term self-indulgence at the expense of long-term well-being. This is how nations and individuals get into debt; this is how economic, demographic, and ecological crises arise. Fortunately for us, it is also how the system will fail to do the only thing that can stop the rise of White Nationalism—until it is too late.

So be of good cheer. If we continue to get our message out, we will win. And internet censorship cannot stop that process. It can only make it slower and more difficult.

Once we win, what should our attitude be toward free speech? Some White Nationalists see free speech as merely a means to take power. I wish to argue that free speech is something that we will want to keep after we win.

Freedom of speech is a value because we are all *fallible* and *vulnerable*. Fallibility means that we can make mistakes. We can have false or inadequate pictures of the world which can be improved upon. Vulnerability simply means that unforeseeable contingencies can upset our best laid plans. To overcome mistakes and misfortunes, we first need to know about them. That means that we need the freedom to be the bearers of bad news. We need freedom of speech, because it makes genuine intellectual and social progress possible.

A society that lacks the ability to change lacks the ability to preserve itself. But a society can't change if it lacks the ability to communicate bad news to its leaders. This is why we should want to protect freedom of speech, even when we are the ones in power.

Why do people oppose freedom of speech? There are two main reasons.

First, some people think they *already* have the truth. This truth is, moreover, absolute: It is complete and not subject to revision. Any contrary position is, therefore, a falsehood. This is why religions in the Abrahamic tradition—including Marxism—have opposed freedom of speech. They claim to be absolutely true. Therefore, all other religions are false—or, at best, semblances of the truth—and must be suppressed.

Second, people with a vested interest in a given political and economic system don't like criticism because it threatens their power and peace of mind.

Both views are irrational.

We all make mistakes. We all suffer misfortunes. But only some of us are destroyed by them. Others learn from them and overcome them. But, again, the first step to overcoming a problem is knowing that one has it.

One of the most powerful ideas of Plato's *Republic* is that political regimes and personality types have analogous structures, so the city can throw light on the soul, and the soul can throw light on the city.

Years ago, I read a listicle on signs that your boss might be a narcissist. The item that made the strongest impression on me is that narcissists tend to punish bearers of bad news.

Defining narcissism is a tricky thing, because we live

in a society in which all manifestations of honor, especially male honor, have been pathologized as narcissism. There is nothing wrong with thinking well of yourself and demanding that others treat you with respect. There is nothing wrong with taking pleasure in praise for your achievements. There is nothing wrong with high self-esteem, as long as it is based on objective merits.

Narcissism is a problem, though, when one puts *preserving a positive self-image* ahead of genuine, positive *self-actualization*.

Everyone makes mistakes. Self-actualization requires that we acknowledge our mistakes, take responsibility for them, learn what we can from them, and then rise above them. The narcissist, however, seeks to preserve his positive self-image at all costs. So when confronted with his mistakes, he denies them and doubles down on them. Or he blames others for his mistakes. Or he goes on the attack, particularly against the bearer of bad news. Anything, really, to avoid taking responsibility and acknowledging that he might have some room to learn and grow.

Narcissists may be highly attractive people. They may have enormous potential. Unfortunately, they think they are perfect just the way they are, and such complacency is deadly to personal growth. So as time passes, you will notice that narcissists seldom actualize their potential. Instead, they come off as dilettantes with a smooth patter. Older narcissists also seem increasingly puerile when compared to their contemporaries.

Narcissists also have difficulty maintaining friendships. Friends tell you what you *need* to hear—even if it is painful. Flatterers tell you what you *want* to hear. Friends aid self-actualization because they will tell you bad news. Flatterers encourage complacency because they only tell you how wonderful you are. Friends threaten a narcissist's positive self-image, whereas flatterers reinforce it.

Obviously it is disastrous to put narcissists into positions of power, because they end up making important decisions based on false or incomplete information fed to them by flatterers. It is no way to run a society.

Today's censorious establishment is narcissism writ large.

By censoring and suppressing White Nationalist ideas, the establishment changes almost nothing. We like to flatter ourselves that the White Nationalist movement is the driving force behind the rise of white racial consciousness. Our enemies share the same illusion. But the main forces behind the rise of White Nationalism are the moral outrages and catastrophic consequences of multiculturalism and white dispossession. People are coming to us in droves less because our movement is *pulling* them than because the system is *pushing* them. Which means that white racial consciousness will continue to rise even if White Nationalists are completely silenced.

Our anti-white oppressors, of course, do not see it that way, for that would threaten their positive self-image. The rise of white identity politics cannot be their fault. So it has to be our fault. They think white identity politics only exists because silver-tongued deceivers like Jared Taylor and Millennial Woes have Twitter accounts. Which is why they conclude that censorship will actually stop us. But White Nationalists are not the cause of ethnic conflict. We are just the bearers of bad news—and advocates of a workable alternative.

Censoring White Nationalists online does not stop people from noticing things, drawing conclusions, and formulating dissenting thoughts. It does not prevent people from discretely communicating their thoughts face to face or organizing in the real world. All censorship does is render the full extent of dissent invisible. This makes it difficult for the establishment to make rational political decisions. Censorship does not make the system stronger; it only makes it blinder, brittler, and more vulnerable. Advocates of censorship are like people who remove the battery from their smoke detector because they are tired of false alarms. But when the house catches fire, you need to know sooner than later.

If I were running a society, I would like to know who the dissidents are and what they think. Thus I would make freedom of speech a fundamental political right. If the dissidents are right, we can learn from them. If they are wrong, we can instruct them. If they are dangerously and stubbornly wrong, we can keep an eye on them.

But if we win, are we really going to give our enemies the freedom to regroup and rebrand, then lead our people back down the road to extinction once more? Don't we want to shut their dirty, lying mouths forever?

There are two points here.

First, if we do come to power, we will have to purge the existing institutions. We will not leave wealth, influence, and political power in the hands of implacable enemies. We will take away their platforms in politics, the media, and the academy. We will just give them early retirements and a lifetime ban on addressing the public. Then we will fill their positions with people who are loyal to us. But that is a far cry from instituting a regime of intellectual censorship.

Second, even if there is a great purge of the existing system, no matter what kind of society you have, in every generation, there will be aberrant personalities who are drawn to ideas that threaten social order. The best way of preventing bad ideas and institutional subversion from taking root again is not to create a world where people have never heard of such things. Instead, we need to create a world where *everyone* has heard of them. A proper education imparts sound information as well as healthy values and tastes. Such an education will inoculate us against bad ideas. We don't have to censor bad ideas if we are immune to them.

Evil will always be with us. But we need not fear it if we are immune to its charms. We should keep evil around, but keep it powerless, as a kind of *memento mori*, a death's head at the feast, so we have a constant reminder of the hell on earth we will vanquish—but only if we start using, and defending, our freedom of speech today.

Counter-Currents, November 6, 2018

THE EUROPEAN FIGHTING SPIRIT

This is my talk from the first Awakening Confer-ence, Helsinki, Finland, April 8, 2018.

"Sing, O goddess, the destructive wrath of Achilles, son of Peleus, which wrought countless woes upon the Greeks, and hurled many valiant souls of heroes down to Hades, and made them prey for dogs and birds . . ." So opens Homer's *Illiad*, the first book of the West. Achilles was the mightiest warrior among the Achaeans. His fighting spirit, however, turned to destructive wrath when he was dis-honored by Agamemnon.

Will the end of the West begin with the words "Refu-gees Welcome" on signs held up by soy-drinking, cuck-mouthed hipsters wrapped in huge scarves, man-purses dangling from their spindly arms, as they stand in train stations frantically signaling their submission to the Koran of globalism and multiculturalism?

Not if we can help it.

I have been asked to speak today on the European fighting spirit. Today's crisis of the West is simultaneously a crisis of nationalism and a crisis of manliness. It is inter-esting that the globalist Left defines both masculinity and nationalism as toxic. What is the connection between masculinity and nationalism? Nationalism is the love of one's people, one's tribe. Nationalism is a partiality to one's tribe over foreigners. Nationalism is the willingness to take one's own side in a fight. And who fights for the tribe?

Men do.

The manly role as warrior is not merely a social con-struct. It is rooted in biology. Men are biologically more inclined to fight. We are more aggressive. We have a

fighting spirit, which is associated with the hormone testosterone. Men are also more physically capable of
fighting. And from a reproductive point of view, men are
more expendable for the survival of the tribe. (A man can
be a father far more times than a woman can be a mother,
so a society can afford to lose far more men in a war than
women.) Thus it is perfectly logical that the globalists who
wish to erase distinct nations and tribes and create a unified and homogenized world have also declared war on
manliness by stigmatizing it and promoting feminism,
androgyny, and confusion about sexual roles and identity.

In recent years there have been alarming reports about
the declining fertility and virility of white and East Asian
men living in advanced industrial societies. These declines
are measured in lowered testosterone and sperm counts.
Various dietary and environmental causes have been proposed for this trend. But not all poisons are chemical.
Mind and body have complex and reciprocal relationships.
Thus it should not surprise us that the relentless psychological war against masculinity might take a physical toll
as well.

The ideological war against manliness is far older than
most of us think. It begins with the modern world itself.
Understanding its deepest roots will light the way to a solution.

Like most narratives in the history of ideas, this one
begins with Plato. In the *Republic*, Socrates divides the
human soul into three parts. There is reason—the faculty
of thought—associated with the head. There is also desire—which seeks the necessities of life, serving the instinct for self-preservation. Desire is associated with the
belly and points below.

We are all familiar with reason and desire. But how
many of us have heard of Plato's third part of the soul?
This is called *thumos*, and it is usually translated as "spirit." But it is not spirit in an immaterial sense, like a ghost.

Instead, it is quite physical. It is team spirit or fighting spirit. Plato locates it in the chest, where we feel anger, where we feel pride.

For Plato, *thumos* is a passionate love of one's own: one's own honor, one's own family, one's own tribe. *Thumos* is always partial, particular, tribal. For Plato and Aristotle—and later Carl Schmitt—*thumos* is the foundation of politics, which always involves partisanship, the distinction between us and them. Women have *thumos* too, but *thumos* is especially connected with manliness, because it is men who fight on the front lines for honor, family, and tribe.

Plato claimed that if there are three parts of the soul, there are three basic kinds of men depending on which part of the soul rules: reason, spirit, or desire. It is possible for there to be conflicts between the different parts of the soul. For instance, your desire might be prompting you to drink too much, but your reason might say "no." Your desire for self-preservation might prompt you to shrink from a fight, but your sense of pride might say no. Your sense of pride might be spoiling for a confrontation, but your reason might veto it because it is strategically sounder to retreat. The part of the soul that tends to win out in such conflicts is the dominant one, and it determines your basic character.

The great German idealist philosopher Hegel argued that *thumos* is the driving force of history. For Hegel, the beginning of history is a duel to the death over honor. Those who put honor above life itself are ruled by spirit. Those who are willing to suffer dishonor to preserve their lives are ruled by desire. The man who puts death before dishonor is free. The man who prefers dishonor to death is a natural slave.

For Hegel, history begins when human beings subordinate life and desire to the higher parts of the soul: reason, imagination, spirit.

Desire is an instinct for self-preservation. *Thumos* is an instinct for self-transcendence, even self-sacrifice. Desire seeks the necessities of life. Reason and *thumos* open up the realm of the non-necessary: of luxury, of the beautiful and useless things that constitute the realm of culture. Of course culture is only "useless" from the point of view of desire. But it has higher uses: It is the medium by which reason and spirit, the distinctly human parts of the soul, express and understand themselves.

Human history is a record of striving for truth and glory. It cannot be understood in purely materialistic terms. And yet most of us today have never heard of *thumos*. We don't really know what honor and patriotism mean. We aren't comfortable with love of one's own—with preferences for our family, tribe, nation, and race. The idea of self-sacrifice seems like an insane form of fanaticism. We are not the same people who fought duels over honor and raised up monuments to heroes.

What has happened to us?

To answer this question, we need to understand the origins of modern liberalism. Plato taught that the city is the soul writ large. Just as an individual can be ruled by reason, spirit, or desire, a society can be ruled by men who follow reason, spirit, or desire.

The ultimate foundation of any political constitution is the moral constitution of the people. Thus to preserve itself, a regime needs to put its stamp on the character of the citizens, and when the character of the citizenry changes, regime change is not far behind.

Before the rise of liberalism, Europe was ruled by an alliance of Throne and Altar. For aristocrats, honor is the highest good. And although Christianity is not exactly a rational worldview, it is a system of ideas that subordinated desire and *thumos* to its imperatives.

The founders of liberalism understood that to overthrow the order of society, they first had to overthrow the order of the soul: to cast down the sovereignty of reason and *thumos* and replace them with the sovereignty of desire.

Reason was demoted from a power that can legislate or create values and turned into a technical-instrumental faculty for satisfying desire. As Thomas Hobbes said, reason is to the passions as "scouts and spies" in service to a general. As David Hume said, "reason is and always ought to be a slave of the passions."

Thumos was dismissed by Hobbes as mere "pride and vainglory." The purpose of liberalism, according to John Locke, was to secure the "industrious and rational" (those who use reason to satisfy their desires) from the interference of the "contentious and quarrelsome" (those who take ideas and honor seriously).

The result of this rewiring of the soul was the rise of modern bourgeois man, for whom material wealth, personal security, and a long life trump all matters of principle and patriotism.

In 2016, America had a hard-fought presidential election in which the central issue was whether preserving the national identity was more important than cheap goods and services. The good guys won by a razor-thin margin. But it is clear that many Americans will not sacrifice a few dollars to save their nation, much less sacrifice their lives.

From an aristocratic point of view, bourgeois man is a natural slave. He will suffer any dishonor as long as he can keep his pension and credit rating. He would rather drop dead on the golf course than die on the field of honor.

Our current rulers are counting on this. Our ethnic displacement depends upon it.

What is the place of manliness in modern bourgeois society? It cannot be abolished altogether. Indeed, the oligarchs will sometimes appeal to it when they need to fight a war. So manliness must be managed. The struggle for honor can be channeled into economic competition, sportsball fandom, and the pursuit of material status symbols.

But for the most part, manliness must simply be suppressed. We are not taught the words we need to understand honor and its role in civilization. The quest for honor is pathologized as "ego" and "narcissism." Spirited boys are diagnosed with ADHD and put on drugs. As C. S. Lewis observed, the modern bourgeoisie are "men without chests." Or, to put it more colorfully, men without balls. There's an empty space where honor and manliness used to reside.

How do we reawaken the European fighting spirit? The first step is to understand what has been taken away from us. Plato's psychology has far more truth and explanatory power than anything offered by Freud or Jung.

Once we have recovered the concept of *thumos* and the language of honor, we will understand that we can be more than clever producer-consumers, natural slaves in the Skinner box economy. We can also be warriors and idealists, people who are willing to fight and die over matters of honor, principle, and patriotism.

To be free, you actually need to know what your options are. Now you know that you have a choice. There is surely no shortage of *thumos* in Finland, the land of black metal, and if you are in this room today, I have no doubt about what kind of men you will choose to be.

Counter-Currents, April 12, 2018

IN PRAISE OF EXTREMISTS

This brief talk was given in London on Friday, May 26, 2017 at the first annual Jonathan Bowden Dinner.

I am currently editing a new collection of Jonathan Bowden's writings called *Extremists: Studies in Metapolitics*.[1] I have edited many hours of transcripts of Jonathan's speeches, and now when I read any of his writings, I hear his voice in my head. I imagine that he would say "Extremists!" like he would bark out the word "glory!"

The book consists of transcripts of Jonathan's lectures on Carlyle, D'Annunzio, Maurras, Heidegger, Evola, Mishima, Savitri Devi, and Maurice Cowling, as well as his speech "Vanguardism: Hope for the Future," all of them delivered at the meetings of the London Forum, the London New Right, and similar events.

All of these speeches illustrate three very important truths that Jonathan visited again and again.

First, metapolitics is important. "Metapolitics" means that which is above or before politics. Political change can only take place if certain metapolitical conditions are met first. Politics is downstream from culture, as Steve Bannon said. Politics follows pretty straightforwardly from our sense of identity—of who we are and where we are going—our sense of right and wrong, and our sense of what is politically possible. If we can alter what our people think about who we are, where we are going, what is morally right, and what is politically possible—then it will be possible for organized nationalist politics

---

[1] Jonathan Bowden, *Extremists: Studies in Metapolitics*, ed. Greg Johnson (San Francisco: Counter-Currents, 2017).

to finally make some headway.

The reason that the political mainstream—both Left and Right—is united in its embrace of multiculturalism and egalitarian leveling is because those ideas are completely hegemonic in the education system, the news media, and the popular culture. The purpose of the New Right is to deconstruct the current anti-white cultural and intellectual hegemony and establish the hegemony of pro-white ideas in its place.

Second, extremists are important. Cultural and political innovations take place on the extremes, at the margins, and then are diffused to—or imposed upon—the mainstream. Thus we should treasure extremists. We should cultivate them. We should encourage their creativity. Then we should steal their best memes and spread them far and wide.

Third, vanguardism is important. We metapolitical radicals must think of ourselves as the vanguard of our people, as a political *avant garde*. We are the ones who must summon our courage, take the risks, blaze the trails, and lead our people toward their salvation.

Vanguardism must be repeatedly emphasized, because the instinct of every politician seems to do the exact opposite. Politicians are inveterate panderers and flatterers of the public mind, which unfortunately has been completely molded by our enemies for generations. Politicians follow the people. Vanguardists seek to lead them. Politicians take public opinion as a given. Vanguardists seek to change it. Politicians always seek to soften their message to appeal to the public. Vanguardists realize this is folly.

If one attracts lukewarm followers who are in only partial agreement, then under normal circumstances, you will be fighting with them as much as with your opponents—and when things get tough, they will sheer off and leave you alone anyway.

Thus vanguardists realize that there is no real substitute for the slow, painstaking, and difficult work of converting a significant minority of our people to our way of thinking. We have to uphold a radical and absolute vision and then bring as many of our people around as possible. We should follow the old Roman maxim, "Suaviter in modo, fortiter in re": suave, supple, and infinitely pragmatic and persuasive in style—yet firm and steadfast, indeed adamantine and dogmatic about essential principles.

Jonathan Bowden died more than five years ago. But vanguardist that he was, he continues to lead us today, through his recordings, YouTube videos, and books, always out there on the extremes, not gone—just gone before.

Counter-Currents, May 29, 2017

IT'S OKAY TO BE WHITE

The Left characterizes the United States and other white countries around the world as systems of "white supremacy" and "white privilege."

White Nationalists claim that the United States and most other white countries are committed to "white genocide": the "great replacement" of whites by nonwhites, which is the predictable consequence of political decisions to promote sub-replacement white fertility, race-mixing, and race-replacement immigration.

Which of these diametrically opposed positions is true?

There's an easy way to find out. In a white supremacist society, you should be able to declare that "It's okay to be white" without controversy or consequences.

Indeed, in a white supremacist society, the only criticism you might receive is for being too tepid. After all, "okay" simply means "adequate but not especially good." It is the equivalent to giving white existence a grade of "C." Being white is apparently nothing to envy, but you wouldn't kill yourself over it either.

When the slogan "It's okay to be white" first appeared on 4chan's /pol/ in 2017, it was promoted as a diagnostic tool to help convince "normies" that we live under anti-white regimes. After all, how could anyone object to "It's okay to be white"?

The slogan does not claim that being white is *great*. It does not claim that being white is *better*. It merely says that being white is *okay*, which is the faintest possible praise. Furthermore, "It's okay to be white" says nothing at all about other races. It certainly doesn't denigrate them.

So on what grounds could one object to saying "It's okay to be white"? As Tucker Carlson put it, "What's the correct position? That it's not okay to be white?"

If multiculturalism is truly an ideology of equality and inclusion, then multiculturalists should have no problem saying "It's okay to be white." They would grant it the same status as "Black is beautiful" and "It's okay to be different." Indeed, whiteness is one form of difference.

Clearly, one could object to a statement as innocuous as "It's okay to be white" *only if one really has something against white people*, specifically a deep hatred or prejudice. This is why it is such a useful diagnostic tool.

"It's okay to be white" flyers and stickers were posted widely in the United States and other white countries, primarily in the Anglosphere. As its creators predicted, the slogan provoked an immediate and intense backlash, far out of proportion to the inoffensive message.

Upon seeing "It's okay to be white" signs and stickers, the first reaction of hundreds of people was to call the police. This can be verified simply by entering the words "police" and "It's okay to be white" in the search engine of your choice. (DuckDuckGo gives the best results.) This happened even in the United States, where the First Amendment to the US Constitution protects freedom of speech. Here are a couple of my favorite headlines:

- ❖ "Sickening to Know People Think Like This"— Police Investigate "It's Okay to Be White" Signs in Scotland
- ❖ 150+ Cases of Outrage, Manhunts over "It's OK to be White," Poster Activist Responds

Indeed, sometimes people deemed these posters too hot for the local cops to handle, so the Federal Bureau of Investigation was called in:

- ❖ FBI probes signs defending white privilege found at Vermont universities

To put this in context, ask yourself how many flyers and stickers you see in a typical day. Dozens? On a university campus, you might see hundreds. Then ask yourself how many times you were tempted to call the police. Most people would have to answer: never. But when hundreds of people saw "It's okay to be white," they were convinced that it is illegal—or that it should be.

Once the police were called, of course the press were alerted, and locals were asked to share their opinions about the flyers. Most people interviewed are certain that "It's okay to be white" constitutes "hate speech," even though it says nothing negative or hateful about anyone.

I'll pull quotes from the first article listed above to give a sense of the sort of statements that are typical: John Swinney, Deputy First Minister of the Scottish Government, declared: "This is atrocious and has no place in Perth or any other part of our country. We must stand together to resist this unacceptable material." Peter Barrett, a Perth councilor, said: "This is despicable hate speech. It is covert racism disguising white supremacist views. People should be in no doubt this is no innocuous joke." Local antiracists claimed that people of color had called to share their feelings. The "terrifying attitudes" expressed by "It's okay to be white" made them feel "sickened," "disgusted," and "unsafe."

My favorite political statement comes from Mayor William Dickinson, Jr. of Wallingford, Connecticut: "whoever posted the signs reading 'It's okay to be white' don't speak for the people of Wallingford," he declared, speaking for the people of Wallingford.

Given that higher education is a citadel of the extreme Left throughout the white world, reactions to "It's okay to be white" on university campuses are especially extreme, as one can see by typing the phrase plus the word "campus" into any search engine. Here are my favorite headlines:

❖ "It's OK to Be White" Flyers Lead to Promise of "Severest Disciplinary Action" by Western Conn. State U.
❖ Ohio universities involve FBI in investigation of "It's okay to be white" and white nationalist group's postings on campus
❖ Oklahoma law school student is questioned by FBI Joint Terrorism Task Force and expelled for posting "It's Okay to be White" flyers on campus

Naturally, university administrators—especially in Podunk schools—can be counted on for the most vehement denunciations of "It's okay to be white." The fulminations of President John Clark of Western Connecticut State University are typical: "I want to state directly and without equivocation that if any member of our university community is found to be party to these revolting actions they will be subject to the severest disciplinary actions, including dismissal as well as possible civil and criminal actions." These are not empty threats. A student at Oklahoma City University School of Law was expelled for posting "It's okay to be white" and ended up talking to the FBI's Joint Terrorism Task Force.

My favorite "It's okay to be white" story is from Australia (75% white), where Senator Pauline Hanson of the nationalist One Nation Party proposed a non-binding statement condemning anti-white racism and declaring "It's okay to be white." Although politicians constantly append their names to all manner of high-minded but empty proclamations, and although not a single Senator in Australia should have had a problem with affirming that "It's okay to be white," the resolution was narrowly defeated on October 15, 2018.

Is any of this behavior consistent with the claim that the United States and other white countries are systems of "white supremacism" and "white privilege"? Obviously not. If we lived in a white supremacist system, people would be *afraid* to call the police about "It's okay to be white" flyers and stickers. College administrators would be *afraid* to threaten students with punishment. Legislators would be *afraid* to vote against "It's okay to be white." But instead, they know that the entire establishment—political, business, media, and academic—is anti-white. Thus it will reward their behavior with an approving pat on the head.

But just how anti-white is this system? Is it really committed to white genocide? One can interpret "It's okay to be white" in at least two ways. The most natural reading is "It's *good* to be white." But the word "okay" is such tepid praise that maybe we should interpret the phrase more along these lines: "It is *acceptable* to be white," or better, "It is acceptable for white people to be, i.e., to exist," or "Don't kill yourself over being white."

A society in which one can be punished for merely asserting that "It is acceptable for white people to exist" is obviously hostile to the very existence of whites. It is a society in which it is *unacceptable* for white people to exist. But if this is true, wouldn't it be natural to explore ways of getting rid of whites altogether? The genocidal implications are obvious.

One might counter that those who object to "It's okay to be white" do not object to the *existence* of white people but merely to *white pride* and *white self-assertion*. Of course, "It's okay to be white" is not a statement of pride and self-assertion. It is absurdly unassuming, almost an apology for existing. But even that is apparently too much self-worth for the preachers of "white guilt" and self-abnegation.

However, even the ideology of "white guilt" is implicitly genocidal. First of all, there is no path to absolution from white guilt. As long as non-whites are unequal to whites, whites will somehow be held guilty. And because inequality is natural, it will always exist. Second, we live in a world of racial strife, in which a race without pride or self-assertiveness—a race burdened with eternal guilt and self-reproach—will fall prey to races without such handicaps.

The best-case scenario is that whites will forever be poisoned with spurious guilt for the inadequacies of others, then milked for free stuff. In short: slavery. The worst-case scenario is outright genocide. And given that violence and instability increase with diversity, orderly factory-farm slavery is the least likely outcome. Thus objecting to white pride—or even mere white "okayness"—is ultimately objecting to white existence as such.

Do the people who object to "It's okay to be white" *consciously* promote white genocide, or do they "know not what they do"? Most of them don't know what they are doing. White genocide is the long-term result of the principles they act on, but most people don't think about the long-term. They unwittingly promote white genocide while thinking they are being moral, pragmatic, or even selfish, because they know that they will be rewarded for anti-white signaling.

The great value of "It's okay to be white" is that when one attacks such banal pro-white sentiments, it brings the implicitly genocidal programing of the Left very close to the surface. If you get hysterical about white people merely existing and not feeling suicidal about it, what do you really stand for anyway?

Of course, the real point of "It's okay to be white" is not to save the souls of anti-whites but to educate ordinary people. This is why we need to keep "It's okay to be white" constantly in the news. The same is true with "All Lives Matter," although "White Lives Matter" is more to the point.

Force the Left to say "It's *not* okay to be white." Force them to say "White lives *don't* matter." And make sure that everyone knows it.

Also, be sure to take down names. If a doctor, lawyer, professor, or politician does not think it is okay to be white, then how can he be trusted to serve the interests of whites? White racists are routinely fired on the assumption that they cannot deal professionally with non-whites. Anti-white racists need to be held to the same standard. A white person would have to be nuts to go under the knife of a surgeon who says "White lives don't matter." We would be foolish to expect anti-white professors to grade us justly. Whites must be protected from such people. It is our job to hold institutions accountable.

When the entire establishment comes together to denounce "It's okay to be white" or "White lives matter," it decisively refutes the Left's thesis that we live in systems of white supremacism and privilege. It also exposes that multiculturalism does not envision a world in which whites enjoy equality and harmony with other groups.

The multiculturalist utopia does not envision whites at all.

Counter-Currents, July 23, 2020

REFRAMING THE
JEWISH QUESTION

When I first became interested in White Nationalism, I noticed that the basic principle of ethnonationalism was always framed as *distinct* from the Jewish question. Ethnonationalism is the idea that racial and ethnic diversity within the same political system are sources of strife, and that peace and harmony are best served by establishing homogeneous sovereign homelands for all peoples.

The Jewish question, however, is supposedly something separate from basic ethnonationalism. It includes such topics as the role of Jews in promoting communism, Zionism, and white decline, and even questions about the holocaust. Some nationalists pursue these questions, but others choose to abstain, merely advocating ethnonationalism but not touching the "JQ."

I wish to suggest that this framing of the Jewish question is entirely wrong. The Jewish question is not something distinct from ethnonationalism. It is not a separate, higher-order, entirely optional set of questions from which ethnonationalists can recuse themselves. On the contrary, the Jewish question is a simple, straightforward application of the basic principle of ethnonationalism.

If ethnonationalism calls for the replacement of multicultural societies with monocultural ones, then Jews, as a distinct people, belong in their own homeland and not scattered among other nations. Thus if England is to be English, Sweden to be Swedish, and Ireland to be Irish, alien populations need to be repatriated to their own homelands, Jews included. That is the ethnonationalist answer to the Jewish question.

This completely accords with the original historical sense of the Jewish question, which is the question of how Jews, being a distinct nation, can be given legal equality and citizenship within other nations. Our answer is: They shouldn't. They belong in their own nation-state. The Jewish question is *entirely* a question about the relationship of ethnicity and nation-states.

The Jewish question long predates such phenomena as communism, Zionism, and the holocaust, so it certainly has no *necessary* connection to them. Nor is the Jewish question *necessarily* connected to the Jewish role in promoting white cultural and demographic decline. Jews could be as venomous as snakes or as innocent as lambs, but there would still be a Jewish question simply because they are a distinct people scattered among other nations.

As far as white ethnonationalists are concerned, the Jewish question is exactly analogous to the black question or the Mexican question or the Gypsy question. Thus the Jewish question is Ethnonationalism 101, not an arcane higher-level elective.

This approach to the Jewish question shifts the burden of proof. It is no longer incumbent on the "anti-Semite" to argue that ethnonationalists need to pay attention to the Jewish question. One does not need to argue that Jews are a "special" people once one observes that they are simply a *different* people, and, therefore, they belong in their own homeland, not among us.

Instead, it is incumbent on those ethnonationalists who would abstain from the "JQ" to explain why Jews, unlike other alien peoples, should have the right to live among us with full rights of citizenship—for this is, in effect, what nationalists who wish to avoid the Jewish question are arguing. When Jared Taylor says Jews "look huwyte to me," he is saying that they are "us," not a distinct nation.

Of course, claiming Jews are "us" is inconsistent with *American Renaissance*'s policy of praising Israel as a nation that protects its borders and takes its own side in ethnic conflicts. For if Jews are just generic white people, then what possible justification do they have for creating an ethnostate on Palestinian land? And if Jews are a distinct people, then they belong in their own homeland, not among other nations. (Technically, Jared Taylor is not a White Nationalist or ethnonationalist because he proposes no solutions.)

Of course, it is easier for Taylor to imply that Jews are "us" in the American melting pot. It would be harder to say that Jews "look Swedish," because they don't. Furthermore, despite high rates of intermarriage, the core of the American Jewish community has remained aloof from the melting pot and strongly identifies with the state of Israel. And finally, Jews aren't generically white to begin with. The racial core of their population is non-European, although some Jews have picked up a lot of European genes in their wanderings.

The Jewish question is not distinct from ethnonationalism. It *is* ethnonationalism applied to Jews. Thus no ethnonationalist is entitled to abstain from it. Once one recognizes that Jews are a distinct people, the ethnonationalist solution to the Jewish question is Jewish nationalism, i.e., Zionism.

Of course many White Nationalists have a whole lot more to say about Jews than merely observing that they are a different people. I have argued that the fate of White Nationalism does not depend one way or another on the outcome of historical debates about the holocaust.[1] But I do believe that Jews are not just *different* from whites, but powerful and malevolent enemies who bear significant responsibility for causing white decline and opposing white renewal.

Some White Nationalists don't want to hear it. But

---

[1] See Greg Johnson, "Dealing with the Holocaust," in *New Right vs. Old Right* (San Francisco: Counter-Currents, 2013).

even so, as I have argued here, they still have to face up to the Jewish question. Because if Jews are nothing more than a distinct people, then ethnonationalists must conclude that Jews belong in their own homeland, not in ours. It is as simple as that.

Counter-Currents, October 27, 2015

WHY THE HOLOCAUST HAPPENED, & WHY IT WON'T HAPPEN AGAIN

As a non-Jew, there are many countries in which I am not free to question the facts of the holocaust or even to offer a definition of what it was. Fortunately, for the purposes of creating white homelands, I don't have to.

I'm not a historian at all, much less a historical revisionist (although I support the freedom of revisionists). I'm a philosopher by training, and my focus is New Right metapolitics, which means establishing the intellectual and cultural preconditions of White Nationalist politics. And, as I have argued in my essay "Dealing with the Holocaust,"[1] whatever happened to Jews in World War II does not impede the case for white ethnonationalism in the least. Indeed, as I shall argue here:

1. The "lesson of the holocaust" that Jews solemnly evoke whenever they can squeeze the slightest financial or political advantage from it, does not actually follow from the holocaust *as Jews define it*.
2. The lesson of the holocaust *as Jews define it* supports rather than impedes the case for White Nationalism.

According to Jews, the lesson of the holocaust is that ethnocentrism and nationalism lead inevitably to genocide against those who are "different," so we need to suppress ethnocentrism and nationalism and embrace multiculturalism and globalism, including race-mixing and open borders. Every time whites show the slightest

---

[1] "Dealing with the Holocaust," in *New Right vs. Old Right*.

ethnic and national self-assertion, the specter of the holocaust is trotted out to put us in our place.

It is implied, of course, that a holocaust could befall anyone who is "different." For instance, now the holocaust is being evoked in discussions about excluding Muslims from white countries. And it is true that any people can be a victim of genocide. For instance, as I have argued elsewhere,[2] whites today are the targets of slow, systematic genocide.

Jewish holocaust propaganda emphasizes the universality of the threat of genocide to build a coalition of people who are against "another holocaust." But the only holocaust such campaigns actively work to prevent is another holocaust *against Jews*. For if every people can fall victim to genocide, then every people should have the right to protect itself: to differentiate and defend itself from others who might destroy it.

But the threat of "another holocaust" is deployed precisely to *prevent* non-Jews from erecting intellectual and political barriers to genocide. It is deployed precisely to reinforce multiculturalism and globalization, which dismantle all intellectual and political barriers preventing Europeans from being demographically swamped by fast-breeding aliens.

The only people who are free to erect barriers against "another holocaust" are Jews.

1. Jews have created a Jewish-supremacist state, Israel, which is dedicated to Jewish survival worldwide.
2. Israel has a mountain of illegal nuclear, biological, and chemical weapons sufficient to deter any attack and to blackmail other coun-

---

[2] Greg Johnson, "White Genocide," in *Truth, Justice, & a Nice White Country*.

tries into doing its bidding.

3.   Jews rigorously police the borders of Israel to prevent unwanted immigrants, just as they subjugate and squeeze out the indigenous non-Jewish population.

4.   Whether in Israel or the Diaspora, Jews encourage a strong sense of "us" vs. "them," which is constantly reinforced in their education—both secular and religious—and popular culture.

5.   Finally, Jews are highly sensitive to preventing threats to their long-term biological survival, including miscegenation, dysgenics, and low fertility.

Jews are a small nation with a tendency toward low fertility and high parental investment (the K-strategy). All such populations are vulnerable to demographic swamping by more fertile, less civilized peoples. But Jews have erected the intellectual and political boundaries necessary for their long-term survival.

Yet Jews routinely claim that they face "another holocaust" whenever whites say "no" to the Jewish state or whenever anti-Semitism shows a tiny uptick. This is utterly ludicrous, because of all low-population, high-K strategy peoples today, *Jews are the least threatened by "another holocaust."* It is also morally obscene when Jews, who are in no danger of genocide, use the specter of "another holocaust" against whites, who are currently the victims of slow genocide.

In short, the "lesson of the holocaust" promoted by Jews is pure self-serving hypocrisy, another "live and let die" double standard: ethnocentrism for Jews but not for us, walls for Israel but open borders for us. The people who are most threatened by genocide need to embrace multiculturalism and open borders, while the people least threatened by genocide can live and travel and make enemies wherever they please, secure in the knowledge that they have an ethnostate with a nuclear arsenal as their protector and refuge. It's a disgusting moral and political swindle, nothing more.

What, then, is the real lesson of the holocaust? To answer this, we first have to know why the holocaust happened.

The answer is simple: The holocaust happened because Jews lived among other peoples rather than in their own homeland. When different ethnic groups live in the same society, ethnic conflict is inevitable. And when ethnic conflicts explode into violence, stateless peoples are much more vulnerable to extermination than those who have sovereign homelands.

However, there will never be another Jewish holocaust. Why? Because the state of Israel now exists, with its vast illicit arsenal of weapons of mass destruction. Adolf Hitler's clone could be elected German Chancellor, and there would not be another holocaust because Jews have nukes and Germans don't.

Thus whenever Jews evoke the possibility of "another holocaust" to extract another pound of flesh from our dying race, the most polite response is to tell them that we have our own holocaust to worry about.

Jews have invested a great deal in promoting the idea that no crime is worse than genocide. Since whites are actually the target of genocide, White Nationalists can use this propaganda to our advantage. The lessons Jews draw from the holocaust—stigmatizing ethnocentrism and nationalism for whites while promoting it for Jews— is morally indefensible. The true lesson of the holocaust is that multiculturalism is bad for everyone, and eth- nonationalism is good for everyone. Jews already have their homeland. Whites need to start reclaiming our homelands and sending non-whites to resettle in theirs.

That is what White Nationalism is all about.

Ethnonationalism for all nations won't create a world without conflict, but it will create a world without holocausts. By replacing multicultural nations with homogeneous homelands for all peoples, ethnonationalism will eliminate ethnic conflicts within states and make it impossible for stateless minorities to fall victim to genocide. As whites approach minority status in our own former homelands, this is a lesson of the holocaust we can all take to heart.

Counter-Currents, March 30, 2016

WHAT IS THE
ALTERNATIVE RIGHT?

The Alternative Right does not have an essence, but it does have a story, a story that begins and ends with Richard Spencer. The story has four chapters.

First the term "Alternative Right" was coined in 2008. Then the *Alternative Right* webzine was launched on March 1, 2010 and ran until December 25, 2013. When it was first coined, the Alternative Right simply referred to an alternative to the American conservative mainstream. When it became the name of a publication, it functioned as a broad umbrella term encompassing such schools of thought as paleoconservatism, libertarianism, race realism, the European New Right, Southern Nationalism, and White Nationalism. By the time the *Alternative Right* webzine was shut down, however, the term Alt Right had taken on a life of its own. It was not just the name of a webzine, but a generic term for Right-wing alternatives to the conservative mainstream.

The second chapter is the emergence in 2014 and 2015 of a vital, youth-oriented, largely online Right-wing movement. This movement encompassed a wide range of opinions from White Nationalism and outright neo-Nazism to populism and American civic nationalism. Thus this movement quite naturally gravitated to the broad generic term Alt Right. The new Alt Right threw itself behind Donald Trump's run for the presidency soon after he entered the race in 2015 and became increasingly well-known as Trump's most ferocious defenders in online battles, to the point that Hillary Clinton actually gave a speech attacking the Alt Right on August 25, 2016.

The third chapter is the Alt Right "brand war" of the fall of 2016. The Alt Right "brand" had become so popular that it was being widely adopted by Trumpian civic nationalists, who rejected the racism of White Nationalists. White Nationalists began to worry that their brand was being coopted and started to push back against the civic nationalists. The brand war ended on November 21, 2016 at a National Policy Institute conference with the incident known as Hailgate, in which Richard Spencer uttered the words "Hail Trump, hail our people, hail victory!" and raised his whiskey glass in a toast, to which some of some of the audience responded with Hitler salutes. When video of this went public, civic nationalists quickly abandoned the Alt Right brand, and the "Alt Lite" was born.

The fourth chapter is the story of the centralization and decline of the Alt Right, largely under the control of Richard Spencer. This period was characterized by polarization and purges, as well as the attempt to transform the Alt Right from an online to a real-world movement, which culminated at the Unite the Right rally in Charlottesville, Virginia on August 11–12, 2017. Both trends led the Alt Right to shrink considerably. Some abandoned the brand. Others abandoned the entire movement. The remnant has retreated back to its strongholds on the internet. As of this writing, there is no fifth chapter, and the Alt Right's future, if any, remains to be seen. Like cancer, there may be no stage five.

THE INVENTION OF A BRAND

The Alternative Right brand first emerged in the fuzzy space where the paleoconservative movement overlaps with White Nationalism. The term "paleoconservatism" was coined by Paul Gottfried, an American Jewish political theorist and commentator. Paleoconservatism defined itself as a genuinely conservative opposition to the heresy of neoconservatism.

The paleoconservative movement was a safe space for the discussion and advocacy of everything that neoconservatism sought to abolish from the conservative movement: Christianity, tradition, America's white identity, an America-first foreign policy, immigration restriction, opposition to globalization and free trade, the defense of traditional/biological sexual roles and institutions, and even—although mostly behind closed doors—biological race differences and the Jewish question.

Aside from Gottfried, the leading paleocons included Samuel Francis, who openly associated with White Nationalists; Joseph Sobran, who was purged from *National Review* for anti-Semitism and who also openly associated with White Nationalists; and Patrick Buchanan, who stayed closer to the political mainstream but was eventually purged from MSNBC for "racism" because his book *Suicide of a Superpower* defended the idea of the United States as a normatively white society.

William H. Regnery II (1941–2021) was a crucial figure in the rise of the Alt Right because of his work in creating institutional spaces in which paleoconservatives and White Nationalists could exchange ideas. Lazy journalists repeatedly refer to Regnery as a "publishing heir." In fact, his money came from his grandfather William H. Regnery's textile business. The conservative Regnery Publishing house was founded by Henry Regnery, the son of William H. Regnery and the uncle of William H. Regnery II. (In 1993, the Regnery family sold Regnery Publishing to Phillips Publishing International.)

In 1999–2001, William H. Regnery II played a key role in founding the Charles Martel Society, which publishes the academic journal *The Occidental Quarterly*, currently edited by Kevin MacDonald. In 2004–2005, Regnery spearheaded the foundation of the National Policy Institute, which was originally conceived as a vehicle for Sam Francis, who died in February of 2005. NPI was run by Louis R. Andrews until 2011, when Richard Spencer took over. Both the Charles Martel Society and the National

Policy Institute are White Nationalist in orientation. *The Occidental Quarterly* is also openly anti-Semitic.

But at the same time Regnery was involved with CMS and NPI, he was also working with Jewish paleocon Paul Gottfried to create two academic Rightist groups that were friendly to Jews. First, there was the Academy of Philosophy and Letters,[1] of which Richard Spencer was reportedly a member.[2] But Regnery and Gottfried broke with the Academy of Philosophy and Letters over the issue of race, creating the H. L. Mencken Club.[3] The Mencken Club, like the Charles Martel Society and NPI, is a meeting ground for paleoconservatives and White Nationalists, although it is also friendly to Jews.

Richard Spencer began as a paleoconservative, entered Regnery's sphere of influence, and emerged a White Nationalist. In 2007, Spencer dropped out of Duke University, where he was pursuing a Ph.D. in modern European intellectual history. From March to December of 2007, Spencer was an assistant editor at *The American Conservative*, a paleoconservative magazine founded in 2002 by Scott McConnell, Patrick Buchanan, and Taki Theodoracopulos in opposition to the neocon-instigated Iraq War. By the time Spencer arrived, however, Buchanan and Taki had departed. After being fired from *The American Conservative*, Spencer went to work for Taki, editing his online magazine *Taki's Top Drawer*, later *Taki's Magazine*, from January of 2008 to December of 2009. Taki thought his magazine was stagnant under Spencer's editorship, so they parted ways. With money raised through Regnery's network, Richard Spencer launched a new webzine, *Alternative Right* (alternativeright.com) on March 1, 2010.

---

[1] https://philosophyandletters.org/

[2] Aram Roston and Joel Anderson, "The Moneyman Behind the Alt Right," *BuzzFeed.News*, July 23, 2017.

[3] http://hlmenckenclub.org/

The phrase "alternative right" first appeared at *Taki's Magazine* under Spencer's editorship. On December 1, 2008, Spencer published Paul Gottfried's "The Decline and Rise of the Alternative Right," originally given as an address at that year's H. L. Mencken Club conference in November.[4] Spencer claims credit for the title and thus the phrase "alternative right," while Gottfried claims that they co-created it.[5] The Alternative Right in decline is, of course, the paleoconservative movement. The Alternative Right on the rise is the more youthful post-paleo movement crystallizing at the Mencken Club and allied forums. The *Alternative Right* webzine was to be their flagship.

The *Alternative Right* webzine had an attractive design and got off to a strong start. I particularly respected Spencer's decision to publish Steve McNallen and Jack Donovan, important writers who were anathema to Christians and paleocons.

But after about six months, the site seemed to lose energy. Days would go by without new material, which is the key to building regular traffic, and matters were not helped by the site layout. Instead of simply putting new material at the top of a blog roll, the site had a host of departments, so one had to click six or eight links to discover that there was no new material. After doing this for a couple of weeks, readers would stop coming, waiting to hear about new material by email or on social media. By the beginning of 2012, Spencer had lost interest in editing the webzine. On May 3, 2012, he stepped down and handed the editorship to Andy Nowicki and Colin Liddell.

---

[4] Paul Gottfried, "The Decline and Rise of the Alternative Right," *Takimag*, December 1, 2008.

[5] Thomas J. Main, *The Rise of the Alt-Right* (Washington, D.C.: Brookings Institution Press, 2018), p. 63; see also my review, "Thomas J. Main's *The Rise of the Alt-Right*," *Counter-Currents*, September 13, 2018.

However, in 2013, Spencer was embarrassed by negative press coverage of one of Liddell's articles and realized that he would always be linked to *Alternative Right*, even though he no longer had control of its contents. On Christmas day of 2013, Spencer shut *Alternative Right* down without consulting or warning Nowicki and Liddell. The domain address was repointed to Spencer's new webzine, *Radix Journal*, which would never become a household name. Then, after another strong start, *Radix* too slumped into a low-energy site.

Nearly four years of articles and comments at *Alternative Right*—the collective contributions of hundreds of people—simply vanished from the web. Nowicki and Liddell salvaged what they could and carried on with the *Alternative Right* brand at BlogSpot.com, although their site had few readers and little influence. In 2018, embarrassed by the decline of the Alt Right brand, they changed the name to *Affirmative Right*.

Spencer's greatest mistake in shutting down *Alternative Right* was not his high-handed manner, which caused a good deal of bitterness, but the fact that he pulled the plug after its name had become a generic term. Just as the brand "Xerox" became a term for photocopying in general, the brand "Hoover" became a verb for vacuuming in general, Sony's "Walkman" became a generic term for portable cassette players, and "iPod" became a generic term for portable mp3 players, the Alt Right had become a generic term for a whole range of radical alternatives to mainstream conservatism. Imagine Xerox rebranding with a weird-sounding Latinate name like Effingo once it had become synonymous with its entire industry.

The beauty of the Alt Right brand is that it signaled dissidence from the mainstream Right, without committing oneself to such stigmatized ideas as White Nationalism and National Socialism. As I put it in an article hailing *Alternative Right* to my readers at *TOQ Online*:

I hope that *Alternative Right* will attract the bright-
est *young* conservatives and libertarians and expose
them to far broader intellectual horizons, including
race realism, White Nationalism, the European New
Right, the Conservative Revolution, Traditionalism,
neo-paganism, agrarianism, Third Positionism, anti-
feminism, and Right-wing anti-capitalists, ecologists,
bioregionalists, and small-is-beautiful types. . . . The
presence of articles by Robert Weissberg and Paul
Gottfried indicates that *Alternative Right* is not a
clone of *TOQ* or *The Occidental Observer*. (Not that
anybody expected that, although some might applaud it.) But that is fine with me. It is more important to have a forum where our ideas interface
with the mainstream that to have another Occidental something-or-other.com.[6]

Obviously, a term as useful as Alternative Right was going to stick around, even after being abandoned by its cre-
ator. Writers at *Counter-Currents*, the *Alternative Right*
BlogSpot site, and even *Radix* kept the concept of the Alt
Right in circulation in 2014 and the early months of 2015,
after which it caught on as the preferred name of a new
movement.

THE EMERGENCE OF A MOVEMENT
The second phase of the Alt Right was quite unlike the
first. The new Alt Right had different ideological origins,
different platforms, and a radically different ethos. But it
rapidly converged on White Nationalism and carried off
some of its best ideas, as well as the term Alt Right. Then
it became an international media phenomenon.
In terms of ideology, the first Alt Right was heavily in-

---

[6] Greg Johnson, "Richard Spencer Launches *Alternative
Right*," *TOQ Online*, March 2, 2010.

fluenced by White Nationalism and paleoconservatism. But the new Alt Right emerged largely from the breakdown of the Ron Paul movement, specifically the takeover of the libertarian movement by cultural Leftists, which drove culturally more conservative libertarians to the Right.[7] Other factors driving the emerging racial consciousness of this group were the Trayvon Martin and Michael Brown controversies, the rise of the Black Lives Matter movement, and the beginning of the migrant crisis in Europe.

The first Alt Right emerged from a milieu of dissident book publishers and print journals, quasi-academic conferences where speakers wore coats and ties, and middle to highbrow webzines. The new Alt Right emerged on social media, discussion forums, image boards, and podcasts, with the webzines coming later. The most influential incubators of the new Alt Right were 4chan and 8chan, *Reddit*, and *The Right Stuff*, especially its flagship podcast, *The Daily Shoah*, and affiliated discussion forums.

The new Alt Right also had a very different ethos and style. While the first Alt Right published reasonable and dignified articles on webzines, the new Alt Right's ethos was emerging from flame wars in the comment threads below. Whereas the first Alt Right cultivated an earnest tone of middle-class respectability, avoiding racial slurs and discussing race and the Jewish question in terms of biology and evolutionary psychology, the new movement affected an ironic tone and embraced obscenity, stereo-

---

[7] In 2009, I predicted that people in the Ron Paul movement would start moving toward white identity politics, so I sponsored an essay contest on Libertarianism and Racial Nationalism at *The Occidental Quarterly*, which I edited at the time, to develop arguments to ease the conversion of libertarians. The essays appeared in *The Occidental Quarterly*, vol. 11, no. 1 (Spring 2011).

types, slurs, and online trolling and harassment.

There were also generational differences between the two Alt Rights. The first Alt Right was the product of a Gen-Xer under the patronage of people born in the Baby Boom and before, who actually had memories of America before the cultural revolution of the 1960s and the massive demographic shifts after 1965, when America opened its borders to the non-white world. The new Alt Right consisted primarily of Millennials and Gen-Zs, some of them as young as their early teens, who were products of a multicultural America with rampant social and familial decay, sexual degeneracy, and drug and alcohol abuse. The first group tended to be conservative, because they had memories of a better country. The latter group had no such memories and tended toward radical rejection of the entire social order.

In 2013, I argued that White Nationalists needed to reach out to significant numbers of white Millennials who had graduated from college during the Obama years, often with crushing debts, and who found themselves unemployed or underemployed, and frequently ended up living at home with their parents.[8] I believed that White Nationalists had better explanations for and solutions to their plight than the Occupy Movement, and this "boomerang generation" could be an ideal "proletariat," because they were highly educated; they were from middle- and upper-middle-class backgrounds; they had a great deal of leisure time, much of which they spent online; and they were angry and disillusioned with the system, and rightly so.

As is so often the case, our movement's outreach gestures went nowhere, but the logic of events drove these

---

[8] Greg Johnson, "The Boomerang Generation: Connecting with Our Proletariat," in *Truth, Justice, & a Nice White Country*.

people in our direction anyway. Boomerang kids became a core group of the new Alt Right known as the "NEETs"— an acronym for "Not in Education, Employment, or Training." When these NEETs and their comrades focused their wit, intelligence, anger, tech savvy, and leisure time on politics, a terrible beauty was born.

The Gamergate controversy of 2014 was an important trial run and tributary to what became the new Alt Right in 2015. Gamergate was a leaderless, viral, online populist insurrection of video gaming enthusiasts against arrogant Leftist SJWs (Social Justice Warriors) who were working to impose political correctness on gaming. Gamergate activists turned the tables on bullying SJWs, brutally trolling and mocking them and relentlessly exposing their corruption and hypocrisy. Gamergate got some SJWs fired, provoked others to quit their jobs, and went after the advertisers of SJW-dominated webzines, closing some of them down.[9]

Gamergate is important because it showed how an online populist movement could actually roll back Leftist hegemony in a specific part of the culture. Although not everyone involved in Gamergate went on to identify with the Alt Right, many of them did. A leading Gamergate partisan, for instance, was Milo Yiannopoulos of *Breitbart*, who later gave favorable press to the Alt Right and is now a prominent Alt-Lite figure. Moreover, Alt Rightists who had nothing to do with Gamergate eagerly copied and refined its techniques of online activism. Indeed, I would argue that Gamergate was the moral and organizational model for the Disney Star Wars boycott of 2018, which

---

[9] For a fuller account of Gamergate, see Vox Day's *SJWs Always Lie: Taking Down the Thought Police* (Castalia House, 2015). See also my review, "Defeating the Left: Vox Day's SJWs Always Lie," in *Confessions of a Reluctant Hater*, second, expanded ed. (San Francisco: Counter-Currents, 2016).

tanked the movie *Solo* and cost Disney hundreds of millions of dollars in lost revenue.

One of the best ways to understand the evolution of the new Alt Right is to read *The Right Stuff* and listen to *The Daily Shoah* from its founding in 2014 through the summer of 2015, when Donald Trump declared his candidacy for the President of the United States. The members of *The Daily Shoah* Death Panel began as ex-libertarians and "edgy Republicans" and educated themselves about race realism and the Jewish question week after week, bringing their ever-growing audience along with them. In February of 2015, Mike Enoch attended the American Renaissance conference and afterwards started calling himself a White Nationalist.

By the spring of 2015, this new movement was increasingly comfortable with the term Alt Right.

When Donald Trump declared his candidacy for the US Presidency on June 16, 2015, most White Nationalist currents found common cause in promoting his candidacy. Trump advocacy encouraged cooperation and collegiality within the movement and provided a steady stream of new targets for creative memes and trolling, and as Trump's candidacy ascended, the new Alt Right ascended with him.

In July of 2015, in the runup to the Republican Primary debates, the new Alt Right scored a major victory by injecting a meme that changed the mainstream political conversation: "cuckservative." The inception of this meme was at *Counter-Currents* when on May 2, 2014, Gregory Hood referred to "cuckold conservatives like Matt Lewis."[10] At this point, many in the media and political establishment realized that a genuine alternative to the main-

---

[10] Gregory Hood, "For Others and their Prosperity," *Counter-Currents*, May 2, 2014; reprinted in his *Waking Up from the American Dream* (San Francisco: Counter-Currents, 2016).

stream Right had arrived.

The new Alt Right became skilled in using social media to solicit attention and promote backlashes from mainstream media and politicians. This attention caused the movement to grow in size and influence, reaching its peak when Hillary Clinton gave her speech denouncing the Alt Right on August 25, 2016.

An older generation of white advocates saw the notoriety of the Alt Right as an opportunity to reach new audiences. Jared Taylor, who was never thrilled with the Alt Right label, wrote about "Race Realism and the Alt Right."[11] Kevin MacDonald wrote about "The Alt Right and the Jews."[12] Peter Brimelow spoke at National Policy Institute conferences. David Duke began circulating memes.

Although I prefer to describe myself with much more specific terms like White Nationalism and the New Right, I always appreciated the utility of a vague term like Alt Right, so I allowed its use at *Counter-Currents* and occasionally used it myself. But whenever I use "we" and "our" here, I am referring to White Nationalism and the New Right, not the fuzzy-minded civic nationalists and Trumpian populists who also came to use the term Alt Right.

Some have dismissed the Alt Right as a Potemkin movement because it was small, existed largely online, and grew by provoking reactions from the mainstream. But this ignores the fact that America is ruled by a tiny elite employing soft power propagated by the media. So if the Alt Right is somehow illegitimate, so is the entire political establishment. The new Alt Right was a perfect mir-

---

[11] Jared Taylor, "Race Realism and the Alt Right," *Counter-Currents*, October 25, 2016, reprinted in Greg Johnson, ed., *The Alternative Right* (San Francisco: Counter-Currents, 2018).

[12] Kevin MacDonald, "The Alt Right and the Jews," *Counter-Currents*, September 13, 2016, reprinted in *The Alternative Right*.

ror image of the establishment media: It was a metapolitical movement that promoted political change by trans-
forming values and perceptions, but it was promoting
change in the opposite direction by negating the establishment's values and worldview.

The Alt Right's particular tactics were dictated by the
asymmetries between itself and the mainstream media.
They had billions of dollars and armies of professional
propagandists. We had no capital and a handful of dedicated amateurs. But new software gave us the ability to
create quality propaganda at home, and the internet gave
us a way to distribute it, both at very little cost. The establishment's vast advantages in capital and personnel were
also significantly negated by the facts that the multicultural consensus it promotes is based on falsehoods and
can only cause misery, and the people who control it are
weakened by arrogance, smugness, and degeneracy. They
are easily mocked and triggered into self-defeating behavior. Our great advantage was telling the truth about liberalism and multiculturalism and proposing workable alternatives. As long as we could stay online, and as long as we
attacked from our strengths to their weaknesses, we went
from success to success.

But many in the movement were not psychologically
ready for success.

BRAND WARS & POLARIZATION

The Alt Right was winning debates and changing
minds. Even more significantly, it was also changing the
parameters of political debate. It was increasingly capable
of driving the news cycle and forcing the political establishment to respond to it. It was also funny, creative, and
cool. Naturally, people wanted to join the movement and
embrace the brand.

But that presented some problems.

First of all, the Alt Right was a decentralized, largely

anonymous, largely online network of individuals, web-zines, and small organizations. Because of its online na-ture, there were no barriers to the movement's viral growth—but by the same token, there were no barriers to entry either.

Second, the Alt-Right brand was effective because of its vagueness. But the flip side of that vagueness was that no-body could control how it was used. Anyone who dissent-ed from the Republican establishment could call himself Alt Right, and as the Trump campaign gained momentum, increasing numbers of young Trumpian populists and civ-ic nationalists wanted to use the term. However, many of these newcomers were ideologically naïve and half-baked.

The main bone of contention was race. The core and vanguard of the Alt Right were White Nationalists. They believed that whiteness is a necessary condition for being a member of any European or European-derived society like the United States. Many newcomers rejected this idea. They were ignorant of the problems of multiracial, multi-cultural societies. They believed the widespread dogma that being an American is a matter of a civic creed, to which people of any race can adhere. Many of them greet-ed White Nationalist ideas with indifference or downright hostility.

The utility of the Alt Right brand was as a tool of reach-ing out to people who were closer to the political main-stream, the "normies." The normies were now coming in droves, and some of them wanted to define the Alt Right in more comfortable civic nationalist terms. This led to a crisis in the Alt Right.

For years, people in our movement had complained about only "preaching to the choir." But now that White Nationalists had a vast audience of people who didn't *al-ready* agree with them, they did not feel elated; they felt threatened. Many people were worried that their move-ment was going to be "coopted" by "entryists" and started thinking in terms of how to repulse newcomers.

I thought this was self-defeating. I urged people to see the situation as an opportunity to convert a vastly expanded audience to White Nationalism. The reason we had come so far is that we had the best arguments and propaganda. We just needed to have faith in ourselves and our message, then we needed to get back in the battle and continue winning new converts.

We also needed to be realistic about the limits of our ability to control a decentralized, grass-roots, online social movement with anything less than the best memes. It is empty to talk of entryism and purges when one is dealing with an online movement with fuzzy boundaries. We cannot prevent people from going online, nor can we throw them off the internet. Finally, we needed to develop an ethos that would allow us to collaborate productively with people closer to the center, whose links to the mainstream were channels for our ideas and influence.

These arguments, however, were rendered moot on November 21, 2016, when Hailgate allowed the mainstream media to forever tie the Alt Right to neo-Nazism. At this point, many civic nationalists rejected the Alt Right brand entirely. This was the birth of the so-called "Alt Lite." It was "lite" only in one sense: It had tossed White Nationalists overboard. The Alt Lite remained a potent force, while the Alt Right became significantly weaker. The Alt Lite commanded a large audience, which White Nationalists could no longer reach. The Alt Lite retained an enormous social network, from which we were now cut off. White Nationalists could accomplish less, because a lot of highly competent and creative people on the Alt Lite would no longer cooperate with us.

Perhaps the worst loss, however, was in the ideological realm. The most important intellectual battle White Nationalists face is to destroy the taboo against white identity politics. After Hailgate, the Alt Lite differentiated itself from White Nationalism by drawing a firm line against white identity politics and digging in behind it, strengthening the taboo among the very people who were most receptive to questioning it.

It was a disaster. But it did get high marks from Andrew Anglin, who had been at the forefront of the effort to identify the Alt Right with Nazism: "Basically, Richard Spencer did something at NPI that was needed exactly right now in the post-victory period: he separated the Alt-Right from the Alt-Cuck and the Alt-Kike. We are better off without these people."[13] We were better off only if one's goal was to assert control over a marginal, subcultural political movement. We were significantly worse off if one's goal was to interface with the cultural and political mainstream and move it in our direction.

Some figures on the Alt Lite have speculated that Spencer engineered Hailgate precisely to drive off civic nationalists by identifying the Alt Right with racial nationalism in its most stigmatized and toxic form. For what it is worth, I ran this theory by someone who socialized and worked closely with Spencer over the years, and he rejected it as "giving him too much credit" for Machiavellian strategizing. Instead, he chalked Hailgate up to a mix of impulsiveness, drunkenness, and unfathomable bad judgment.

Whether Hailgate was intentional or not, however, it became the pattern for what came next: a drive to centralize the Alt Right under the leadership of Richard Spencer, which led to further division and dysfunction.

CENTRALIZATION, PURGES, & BREAKDOWN

It was quite natural for Richard Spencer to regret dropping a brand that had been adopted by a potent polit-

---

[13] Andrew Anglin, "Jared Taylor Throws Richard Spencer Under the Bus," *Daily Stormer*, November 27, 2016.

ical force and an international media sensation. So he attempted to reassert ownership. But there was a problem: the new movement that emerged in 2014 to 2015 owed little to Spencer except the name that it eventually adopted. Spencer acknowledged this in an October 12, 2016 interview he gave to political scientist George Hawley who was doing research for his book *Making Sense of the Alt-Right*, where Spencer says, "The Alt Right is what it is today not because of me; it is what it is today because I let it go."[14] This is correct.

But from the point of view of 2018, it is also true to say that the Alt Right is the mess it is today—largely but certainly not entirely—because Spencer tried to take it back.

On September 9, 2016, NPI held a "What is the Alt Right?" press conference in Washington D.C. The speakers were Richard Spencer, Jared Taylor, and Peter Brimelow. At the conference, Spencer unveiled his "Alt Right logo," which never really caught on.[15] Clearly Spencer wanted to get out ahead of the new Alt Right, redefine it in his terms, and put his stamp on it.

After Hailgate, Richard Spencer and Persian-American academic Jason Reza Jorjani, who also spoke at NPI 2016, began a series of meetings to create what became the Altright Corporation. The main shareholders were Richard Spencer, Jason Jorjani, Daniel Friberg of Arktos Media, and Red Ice TV.[16]

The Altright Corporation launched the *AltRight.com* webzine on January 16, 2017. Spencer's plan was to elevate

---

[14] George Hawley, *Making Sense of the Alt-Right* (New York: Columbia University Press, 2017), p. 68.

[15] See Margot Metroland, "The NPI Presser: 'What is the Alt Right?,'" *Counter-Currents*, September 12, 2016.

[16] On some of the shady, deep-state connected operators who encouraged the formation of the Altright Corporation, see Greg Johnson, "The Alt Right Corporation and the American Deep State," *Counter-Currents*, October 18, 2017.

himself to movement leadership by *looking like* the leader. He was going to "fake it till you make it"[17] by coaxing as many important voices as possible onto his platform; by coopting organizations like Identity Evropa; by schmoozing with the players who were too big to be coopted (TRS, Jared Taylor, Kevin MacDonald, Peter Brimelow); by maligning and purging those who were immune to his charms (Milo, Mike Cernovich, me); and, above all, by giving interviews to the mainstream media on the cynical but unfortunately correct assumption that *many people in our movement will accept whomever the enemy media anoints as their leader.*

The new webzine followed the same pattern as Spencer's other webzines: a strong start and then a slump. Only in this case, the start was much weaker and the slump came much sooner. *AltRight.com* also differed from Spencer's earlier webzines in the gutter vulgarity of its writing, which was clearly an attempt to curry favor with chan kids and *Daily Stormer* readers. For instance, this is how Vincent Law concludes his article "Daniel Borden Did Literally Nothing Wrong":

> . . . in the case of Daniel, inside sources say that he is holding up well. He has already received hundreds of nude photos and marriage proposals from girls solidly in 7–8 HB range. There is even a smattering of 9s as well.

---

[17] In Josh Harkinson's "Meet the White Nationalist Who Wants to Ride the Trump Train to Lasting Power," *Mother Jones*, October 27, 2016, Spencer is quoted as follows: "'I still feel like we are faking it until we make it,' he confesses. 'I mean, in some ways, you've got to fucking fake it. You have to project success and project power and kind of make it a self-fulfilling prophecy . . .'" Spencer has never disputed the accuracy of this quote, and it coheres with his pickup artist *schtick* that the model for political persuasion is "seduction."

Daniel is worried though.

He says he doesn't know how to swim and has no idea how he won't drown once he gets out [of jail] from swimming in all that pussy. Don't worry, Daniel. We'll be waiting with some water wings once you get out.[18]

Serious writers were not exactly clamoring to share the same platform.

Spencer's efforts at polarization and purges were no more successful. It is a classic White Nationalist rookie move for a new, would-be leader to set up his PO Box and webzine and then to try to recruit followers and donors by launching attacks on his rivals. The underlying assumption of the polarization strategy is that a certain percentage of followers will come over to the attacker's camp, while the rest will remain with the target. But the movement as a whole will not suffer. The deck will simply be reshuffled.

In fact, such tactics are profoundly damaging to the movement as a whole. To use arbitrary numbers, the attacker might gain 15% of the target audience, and the target might retain 40 to 50%, depending on his response. But the rest become disgusted and demoralized and refuse to have anything to do with either party. Some simply quit entirely. Polarization, therefore, brings some benefits to the aggressor but harms the movement as a whole, which is why we should shun anyone who uses this strategy as a selfish self-promoter.

One can argue that subjecting a movement like the Alt Right to any kind of centralized leadership is a bad idea. The Alt Right—and White Nationalism as a whole—is a decentralized, non-hierarchical network. The nodes of

---

[18] Vincent Law, "Daniel Borden Did Literally Nothing Wrong," *Altright.com*, July 9, 2017.

this network are individuals—most of them anonymous—and small hierarchical organizations. These nodes are largely linked by the internet, especially social media platforms.

The drivers of the movement are creative individuals who produce memes in the form of articles, podcasts, videos, and images. When a particularly potent meme is created, the network propagates and augments it until the meme is exhausted and something new comes along. When it works well, the movement is endlessly stimulating and fun, and it has genuine transformative effects on the public mind.

Because the network makes possible the creative collaboration of countless anonymous individuals, one can argue that the network itself is actually smarter, more creative, and more powerful than any of the nodes. There are differences between the nodes. Some create memes; others merely propagate them. Some individuals and organizations have larger audiences, greater impact, and more moral and intellectual credibility than others. I would like to see many large, well-funded, and highly influential companies, think tanks, and political parties emerge from this network. But even the biggest nodes are smaller than the network as a whole.

What would happen to the overall effectiveness of the network if a would-be leader tried to subject it to his control? Even a small networked movement like the Alt Right is more complex and creative than any individual node. Thus if an individual were to try to assume leadership of the movement, he would inevitably have to simplify its structure, which would inevitably dampen its creativity and power. This is why centralization is always accompanied by polarization and purges. The size and complexity of the movement has to be reduced to what can be comprehended and controlled by an individual mind. The smaller the mind, the greater the damage. Those who are unimpressed with the would-be leader must, furthermore, be driven out.

The quest for centralization might promise immense ego gratification for a would-be leader. But the net result is a smaller, dumber, less creative movement. It is also less active, because formerly independent agents must now wait around for orders from above. Or they have to wrangle to gain the agreement of others, whereas formerly they could just act on their own judgment. Thus centralization inevitably makes the movement weaker. This would be true even if the centralizer were the kind of organizational genius capable of founding a large corporation or a government. It is especially the case when the would-be leader can't even run a successful webzine.

Spencer's attempts to purge rivals from the movement were also unsuccessful but created a great deal of lasting collateral damage. In the fall of 2016, Spencer's polarization and purge tactics consisted largely of whispering campaigns. After Hailgate, he unleashed a barrage of transparently envious and embittered tweets against Milo, Cernovich, and other Alt-Lite figures.

But on June 1, 2017, Spencer tried something much bolder. Spencer launched an attack against me and *Counter-Currents* with a lame and dishonest article co-authored by Daniel Friberg, "Greg Johnson's Attacks and How to Deal with Them."[19] He did not, however, reckon any blowback into his plans. *Counter-Currents* is still here, but the Altright Corporation began to unravel at that point, first losing Jason Jorjani then Red Ice. Eventually

---

[19] See Greg Johnson, "Reply to Daniel Friberg," *Counter-Currents*, June 18, 2017; Omar Filmersson, "Greg Johnson Told the Truth," *Counter-Currents*, June 22, 2017; Alan Smithee, "Friberg Falls Back," *Counter-Currents*, June 25, 2017; John Morgan, "The Truth About Daniel Friberg," *Counter-Currents*, June 27, 2017.

even Friberg quietly severed ties.

But nobody really wins such battles. In this case, many relationships of friendship, comradeship, and collegiality were replaced by enmity, bitterness, and distrust that persist to this day. Connections that allowed productive collaborations were severed, leaving the movement less effective and more dysfunctional.

Spencer's use of the media to elevate him to leadership status was ultimately unsuccessful as well. The media attention Spencer received came at a price. All Spencer had to do was help the media advance its anti-white agenda by conforming to one of its negative stereotypes, in Spencer's case the smug, snobbish, amoral WASP plutocrat.[20] The media loved Spencer, because he helped them make White Nationalism look bad. Spencer loved the media, because he hoped it would elevate him over his rivals in the movement. Neither party to this cynical transaction had any interest in representing White Nationalism in a way that might actually connect with the white majority.

As I have already argued, there is no way to be the leader of this movement as a whole. But one can still aspire to be a leader *within* the movement. There are basically two ways to do this: the grassroots way and the AstroTurf way. The grassroots way is to build a solid platform from the ground up, based on a record of achievements, whether they be in political activism or propaganda work. But the grassroots way is also the hard way, requiring many years of sustained and patient labor.

Thus it is tempting to take the easy way, the AstroTurf way: give an interview, or pull a publicity stunt, in the hope that the enemy media will anoint you leader. But even if you pull it off, you can't remain a *virtual* leader for-

---

[20] For more on the press engagement strategy of Spencer and Matt Heimbach/Matt Parrott, see Greg Johnson, "In Bed with the Press," *Counter-Currents*, March 6, 2018.

ever. You have to start delivering *actual* results, *positive* results. Spencer has done things of value over the years: NPI conferences, *Radix*, and Washington Summit Publishers. But these were all sidelined for rallies and a college speaking tour that turned out to be net negatives.

As of the end of 2018, most of Spencer's followers have abandoned him, even his inner circle, and he has gone silent except for an occasional Tweet or YouTube livestream. The establishment, then, got the better deal. Whether Spencer ultimately fades away or makes a comeback, the media will be trotting out footage of Hailgate and other cringe-inducing gaffes to stigmatize Trump and White Nationalism for decades to come.

Those of us who are trying to present a morally coherent and historically accurate case for white self-determination will be forever dogged with clips of Spencer defending imperialism and white supremacism, attacking freedom of speech, calling for the genocide of Turks, dismissing the relevance of morality, and playing "agree and amplify" with outrageous anti-white canards like "Part of your greatness is the exploitation of other people."[21] It would be one thing if these were sincere but mistaken convictions. But with Spencer they are simply half-baked postures and provocations.

One cannot, however, entirely blame Richard Spencer for the declining fortunes of the Alt Right. Again, the movement that emerged in 2014 and 2015 owed little to Spencer except its name. And even though Spencer damaged the Alt Right by trying to assert control over it, the movement—including its problems—was always bigger than him. Which means that he cannot bear sole blame for its downfall. In particular, it is unjust to blame Spencer for the disastrous Unite the Right Rally of August 11–12, 2017, since he played little role in planning it. There were

---

[21] https://youtu.be/h6N4VNxDT24

broader forces at work, in which Spencer himself was caught up, and which can be summed up as *the return of White Nationalism 1.0.*

WHITE NATIONALISM 1.0 & 2.0

In 2015, when the new Alt Right became more comfortable with the idea of White Nationalism, most of its members had only the vaguest acquaintance with an earlier generation of White Nationalist figures. Lawrence Murray, for instance, claimed, "I myself had never heard of [William] Pierce and [David] Duke . . . until becoming involved with the Alt-Right."[22] Murray's experience is typical of Millennial and Gen-Z Alt Rightists.

The Alt Right began calling the White Nationalism of their fathers' generation "White Nationalism 1.0." They dubbed the Alt Right "White Nationalism 2.0." Built into this framework was a dismissive attitude toward White Nationalism 1.0 and an assumption that the Alt Right was a marked improvement. I agreed with the latter judgment. But more often than not, Alt Rightists dismissed figures like Pierce and Duke based simply on impressions gleaned from the mainstream media. I thought it was shameful to parrot enemy propaganda. Thus when such attitudes appeared in various private forums, I urged Alt Rightists to become better informed and learn what they could from White Nationalism 1.0. As a movement, it was largely a failure, but learning from failure is part of success. Unfortunately, some people learned the wrong lessons.

By the beginning of 2017, I began to notice a definite shift toward 1.0 ideas and attitudes:

❖ The assumption that National Socialism is the only authentic form of White Nationalism

---

[22] Quoted in George Hawley, *Making Sense of the Alt-Right,* p. 80.

- ❖ Advocating the mass extermination of non-
  whites, race-mixers, and homosexuals, straight
  from the pages of *The Turner Diaries*
- ❖ A marked upsurge of attitudes toward women
  that can legitimately be labeled misogyny, including the toxic "white *sharia*" meme and a
  push to bully female voices into silence
- ❖ A revival of the skinhead subculture of binge
  drinking and hard drugs
- ❖ The return of costumed demonstrations and
  street brawls with Leftists

The entirely negative consequences of these attitudes and
behaviors were easy to predict. But they were nevertheless
tolerated, given platforms, and even advocated and encouraged by leading Alt-Right voices.

First and foremost, WN 1.0 ideas are self-marginalizing
and self-defeating.

The best possible way to advocate White Nationalism
is to emphasize that it is a political philosophy based in
human nature, confirmed by social science and political
experience, and rooted in the political traditions of all
white nations. The worst possible way to advocate White
Nationalism is to claim that every form of ethnonationalism is fake—except the German form that was defeated in
1945 and has been execrated continuously since then.[23]

As I argue in *The White Nationalist Manifesto*, the
white race is currently being subjected to genocide, and
White Nationalism is the best political system to end
white genocide and restore healthy white communities.[24]
The worst possible way to rally our people against the
genocide directed at us is to advocate genocide against

---

[23] See Greg Johnson, "The Relevance of the Old Right," *The
White Nationalist Manifesto*.

[24] See Part 1, White Nationalism, encompassing chapters 2–7.

others.

One of the self-evident axioms of politics is that a movement has a better chance of winning if more people fight for it and fewer people fight against it. There are two ways to do this. First, we must rally our own people to our banner. Second, we can try to split the enemy bloc by converting some of them to allies, sympathizers, or simply neutral parties.

But if we have exterminationists among us, our own people will not side with us, because such morally repugnant positions only attract psychopaths to the movement while repulsing normal people. Indeed, exterminationists actually reinforce the white guilt propaganda that asserts that whites are a uniquely evil race whose disappearance would be no great loss to the cosmos. Furthermore, exterminationists ensure that the enemy bloc will be larger and more unified simply because no non-white in his right mind could sympathize with or be indifferent to our movement—much less aid it.

Just as egalitarians label simple realism about racial differences "hate," they label simple realism about the differences between the sexes "misogyny," i.e., the hatred of women. That said, however, there are quite a few race realists who genuinely hate other races, many of them gleefully, without reluctance or reservations.[25] Likewise, there are quite a lot of people in our circles who simply hate women.

Many of the race-haters don't understand that the fundamental purpose of our movement is to drain the multicultural swamp in which racial hatred breeds, rather than to self-indulgently wallow in it. Indeed, the more the movement is simply a platform for expressing hate, the less likely it is to actually create a society that is free of

---

[25] See, by way of contrast, Greg Johnson, "Confessions of a Reluctant Hater," in *Confessions of a Reluctant Hater*.

racial hatred.

Likewise, many of the woman haters don't understand that another fundamental aim of our movement is to drain the cultural swamp that breeds distrust and hatred between the sexes, rather than just to provide a platform for misogynists to vomit bile into the void. Indeed, the more the movement is simply a safe space for damaged people to vent, the less likely it is to actually create a society with healthy families and sexual norms.

Politics is not therapy. The more our movement resembles a group therapy session—with the lunatics running the asylum—the less likely it is to achieve its political goals.

The idea of "white *sharia*" took wholesome and salutary truths about the differences between the sexes and their appropriate roles in the family and society at large and self-defeatingly packaged them in terms that bring to mind child brides, arranged marriages, rape gangs, sex slavery, polygamy, clitoridectomies, acid attacks, *purdah*, and dressing in bedsheets.[26]

Again: the White Nationalist movement has a better chance of winning if more people fight for us and fewer people fight against us. Thus it is self-defeating for a movement that is already small and marginal to launch bullying campaigns against entire classes of white people who want to help—including the more than 50% of the white race that happens to be female.

As I argue in my essays "Redefining the Mainstream" and "Against Right-Wing Sectarianism," both reprinted below, White Nationalism will win when it becomes the common sense of the whole cultural and political mainstream. There is nothing inherently Right-wing about the essential ideas of White Nationalism: for instance, that

---

[26] See Donald Thoresen, "Whigger *Sharia*," in *The Alternative Right*.

being white is a necessary condition of European identity; that the white race is being subjected to slow genocide due to policies that promote low white fertility and non-white immigration; that creating sovereign white homelands with pro-natal, pro-family values is the solution to white genocide; and that Jews have played a leading role in promoting white genocide and blocking whites from stopping it. At present, though, White Nationalism is a movement of the Right. But that presents us with a tricky problem.

To transform the mainstream in a White Nationalist direction, we need to let our message emerge from its current Right-wing cocoon and spread its wings. It would be self-defeating to change any of our essential principles to conform to the mainstream. The whole point is to get the mainstream to conform to us. Thus the only thing we can change is how we *package* and *communicate* our message. We need to craft versions of the essential White Nationalist message that can convert every white constituency. We even need to convert some non-whites into allies and sympathizers, or at least convince them they have nothing to lose from our victory.

That is a tall order, and we are just beginning to figure out how to make it work. It is, however, easy to determine what won't work, namely insisting that the White Nationalist idea must be accepted with a long list of Right-wing add-ons. Right-wing sectarianism is the path to self-marginalization and self-defeat, and in this game, White Nationalism 1.0 is the undisputed champion.

But we know that victory is possible, because it was not too long ago that pro-white ideas were culturally and politically dominant. Furthermore, the present hegemony of anti-white ideas was created through the exact same metapolitical strategies by which we aim to reverse it. The sooner we stop doing things that don't work—and start doing things that do work—the sooner we win.

We need to take a nuanced stance on drinking, drugs, and other unhealthy habits. On the one hand, our movement aims at the creation of a better society. On the other hand, the people in our movement are the products of the profoundly sick society that we wish to overcome. Thus young audiences find it real and relatable to watch Millennial Woes chain-smoking his way through his YouTube videos, or to listen to the countless podcasts whose hosts and guests are obviously drunk or stoned.

But imagine tuning back in ten years from now and finding them doing the exact same thing. Obviously, something would have gone terribly wrong. Obviously, an important opportunity would have been lost. For the whole point of being real and relatable is to establish a connection to one's audience in order to *lead* them. Not just to lead them, to *better* them. But we cannot better people if we do not better ourselves. Thus an ethos that celebrates or merely tolerates chemical dependencies is self-defeating. It turns the movement into just another dead-end of modern decadence rather than an exit from it. How can we overcome the downward plunge of the whole modern world if we can't even overcome the downward pull of our own petty vices?

Imagine, for a moment, that the movement adopted Harold Covington's General Order Number 10: for the duration of the struggle, no White Nationalist will use alcohol and drugs.[27] We would gain much and lose nothing. First, drugs and alcohol impair judgment and effectiveness, leading to bad decisions and clumsy execution with

---

[27] See Greg Johnson, "Birth of a Nation: On Harold Covington's Northwest Quartet," in *In Defense of Prejudice*, and "Drug Legalization in the White Republic," in *Confessions of a Reluctant Hater*, a libertarian position that I have abandoned because of the catastrophic consequences of drugs on white communities.

predictably self-defeating consequences. Second, drugs and alcohol get people into trouble with the law, which is one way they are turned into informants and saboteurs. Third, drugs and alcohol consume time and money that could be better spent on the cause. Fourth, demanding people give up drugs and alcohol communicates that our cause is serious and demands personal sacrifices but also makes us better and nobler people. Finally, adopting a zero-tolerance policy for drugs and alcohol weeds out unserious people who prize personal self-indulgence over racial salvation. Now imagine if the Alt Right had adopted this sort of ethos at the beginning of 2016. Think of everything we could have avoided.

We also need to take a nuanced stance on the return of costumed protests and brawls with communists. The Old Right began by battling communists in the streets of Europe. For a while after Trump's election, it looked like those days were back as masked communists ("antifa") attacked Trump supporters in the streets. Naturally, Trump supporters, including White Nationalists, wanted to fight back. It was only natural to test the waters and see what was possible.

At a certain point, however, caution and prudence were tossed to the winds. People got giddy, grandiose, and delusional. For instance, in the midst of the Unite the Right rally in Charlottesville, Richard Spencer declared, "The Alt-Right is finished debating, negotiating, surrendering. We're ready to close ranks and fight for what is ours. . . . We stand poised to conquer the continent."[28] In fact, the Alt Right stood poised for nothing but a fall: a wave of doxing, deplatforming, and criminal and civil trials, the costs of which will continue to mount for years to

---

[28] Quoted in Brett Barrouquere, "Judge upholds bulk of lawsuit against alt-righters in Charlottesville after 'Unite the Right,' dismisses Peinovich," *Hatewatch*, July 10, 2018.

come.

Charlottesville offered valuable lessons that many of us took to heart. Don't hold rallies in enemy strongholds. Don't announce our events months in advance, giving the enemy time to prepare. Don't trust the enemy media to convey our message. Don't trust police to enforce the laws if they benefit us. White Nationalists will be fired from their jobs, demonized by the press, deplatformed from the web, and prosecuted by the anti-white establishment, while antifa will be coddled. We don't have the numbers, money, institutions, and public sympathy to engage in demonstrations like Unite the Right. The Left has effectively bottomless reserves of lawyers and money to harass us with frivolous lawsuits, the aim of which is to exhaust and bankrupt us, and to expose the identities of our activists and donors through the "discovery" process. But we don't have comparable resources to defend ourselves.

The great lesson of Charlottesville was simply to take stock of the strengths and weaknesses of both the establishment and our movement, then focus on doing what works. The enemy's strengths include vast numbers of people, effectively infinite amounts of money, and control over the leading institutions of society. The same can be said, however, of any establishment right up to the point that it was overthrown. The enemy's chief weaknesses are promoting morally heinous and socially destructive policies based on lies, as well as being corrupt, decadent, vicious, and silly.

Our weaknesses are the mirror image of our enemies' strengths. Our movement has tiny numbers and scarce funds. We control almost no institutions of our own and are at the mercy of the institutions controlled by our enemies. Again, this is true of practically every revolutionary movement at one time or another, including those that go on to win.

Our strengths, too, are the mirror image of our enemies' weaknesses. They are promoting policies based on lies about human nature that are leading to hatred, conflict, and eventually genocide. We promote policies based on truths about human nature that will minimize ethnic conflict, hatred, and genocide. They promote bad arguments and double standards, and we are masters of deconstructing them. They are laughable, and we are masters of mocking and shaming them.

As long as we attacked the enemy's weaknesses from our strengths, we were making remarkable metapolitical gains. But as soon as some attacked the enemy's strongest points from a position of relative weakness, they were destroyed. Those of us who are still in the struggle either never got involved with street activism or have returned to doing what works: metapolitics—which means community organizing and the propaganda war, including the low-risk, high-reward propaganda of the deed strategies pioneered by the Identitarian Movement and adopted by Identity Evropa in the United States.

***

Is the story of the Alt Right over, or will there be a next chapter? At this point, we shouldn't really care. Even if the Alt Right is dead, White Nationalism and white identity politics are very much alive, and it is the issues not the symbols that really matter. The Alt Right was just a brand. It was a useful umbrella term that created a discursive space in which White Nationalists could network with and convert people who are closer to the mainstream. But Richard Spencer collapsed that discursive space with Hailgate. The much-reduced Alt Right movement that Spencer created under his leadership met its Waterloo at Charlottesville. At this point, the Alt Right movement is dead, and the brand has been irreparably tarnished. There will always be some people who will choose to call themselves Alt Right, just as there are people who call them-selves Nazis, i.e., it is little more than a defiant gesture of self-marginalization. Those who are serious about creating a future for white people need to look beyond the Alt Right toward a new nationalism.

Counter-Currents, October 10, 18, & 22
& November 15, 2018

AGAINST RIGHT-WING SECTARIANISM

It is important for White Nationalists to visualize what victory would look like. There are really two answers to this question. The ultimate answer is our vision of Whitopia, the society we want to create. But before we build Whitopia, we need to achieve a victory over the present political system. This victory will give us the power to create our ideal society, and it may come decades before Whitopia is realized.

Victory, like everything, depends on things we can control and things we can't control.

The things we can't control can be summed up under the rubric of "the historical moment," which includes all objective social conditions, including unpredictable historical contingencies like the election of Donald Trump. The historical moment can be either auspicious or inauspicious for our plans. The best-organized movement in the world will make no headway if the historical moment is not right. On the other hand, if we do nothing, our plans will never be realized, no matter how receptive the historical moment might be.

The things we can control are all the things we can actually do, and for our purposes they boil down to political and metapolitical activism. Political activism encompasses all attempts to gain control over the levers of political power. Metapolitical activism encompasses creating the conditions necessary for political success. There are two branches of metapolitics: organizing a White Nationalist community and propaganda, i.e., creating ideas and media to impart a pro-white worldview.

The way that politics and metapolitics work together can be appreciated by considering them in isolation.

It is possible to gain power over a society by purely political activity, without persuading the general public of the rightness and feasibility of our ideas. The clearest example of this path is a foreign invasion, in which the apparatus of state is seized, and all opposition quelled, simply by force. Another such model is an unpopular revolution from within, in which an armed militant party seizes control of the state. Such a route is, of course, maximally difficult and costly, simply because victory becomes easier when more people agree with you and fewer people fight against you. Decreasing the numbers of your enemies and increasing the numbers of your friends and allies is the work of metapolitics.

It is also possible to gain power over a society by purely metapolitical means, simply by persuading the overwhelming majority of the population that one's ideas are correct. If White Nationalism became the common sense of a whole society, then one would not need to organize a White Nationalist party and take control of the state, for *all* the political parties would effectively be White Nationalist. No matter how vehemently the different parties might disagree about issues like taxes, health care, and feminism, white identity and interests would be sacrosanct, and this attitude would extend through the whole of the culture. At that point, from the point of view of white interests, it would not matter what political party ends up in charge, because whites simply cannot lose.

This full-spectrum metapolitical dominance is what I call "hegemony." Hegemony means rule from afar. In politics, a hegemon is a power that dominates subordinate powers without directly ruling them. For instance, the United States is hegemonic throughout Europe and the Western hemisphere, although its clients are sovereign states. In metapolitics, hegemony means a broad cultural consensus sets the parameters of political debate and decision-making, framing every issue in "heads I win, tails you lose" terms, so that no matter what the political outcome, the hegemonic values continue to reign.

In the white world today, the organized Jewish community exercises cultural and political hegemony. Thus no matter how divided the mainstream might be on specific issues, it is united in treating Jewish sensibilities and interests as sacrosanct. The goal of the North American New Right is to deconstruct this Jewish hegemony and replace it with a similar hegemony of pro-white ideas. Wouldn't it be nice, for a change, if white identity and interests were sacrosanct in white countries?

In practice, of course, the political and metapolitical paths to power work in tandem. Even an armed takeover by a revolutionary party would presuppose metapolitics in order to create an ideological consensus within the party itself. And even if White Nationalism became the common sense of the whole society, we would seek to make that victory permanent by organizing to take control of governments and other institutions and oust anti-whites from all positions of power and influence.

With these concepts in mind, we can now return to visualizing our victory over the present cultural and political powers, so as to clear the way to building a White Nationalist society. Keeping in mind that politics and metapolitics can never be fully separated, we can still ask if our victory will be *primarily* political or metapolitical. My answer is: *our victory must be primarily metapolitical.*

To appreciate this point, take a look at the present state of the Trump administration. Through organizational genius and the sheer force of personality, Donald Trump managed to rouse a populist revolt against the entire political, intellectual, and media elite. This revolt placed him in the White House by a razor-thin margin. Although Trump has the loyalty of the white majority, the voters do not exercise day-to-day control over the levers of cultural and political power. Instead, those are in the hands of people who fundamentally disagree with Trump's outlook and agenda. Trump won a political victory, but in terms of metapolitics, the globalists are still very much in power. Their ideas are hegemonic, and their networks of influence extend throughout society, blocking Trump at every turn. To push his political agenda through, Trump also needs a metapolitical sea change. He needs a community of people who agree with his populist vision, who can win new people to his cause, and whose influence can counter the globalist network. It is our job to create it.

Trump, moreover, is a far cry from a White Nationalist. The opposition he faces is nothing compared to what would greet a White Nationalist if, by some miracle, he could be elected President in the first place.

A White Nationalist will never attain effective political power in the United States or any other white nation until we change the culture. We have to convince a very high percentage of our people that White Nationalism is both morally right and politically feasible. We also have to convince a significant percentage of those who are ambivalent about us that we are still a legitimate political force, perhaps even worthy political allies. Then we need to convince a large percentage of those who oppose us to do so passively rather than actively. And only at that point will we be able to gain state power and use it to disempower, silence, and marginalize the anti-whites who remain.

The metapolitical approach also plays to our strengths. Right now, the enemy has complete control of all the commanding institutions of our society. Their weakness, however, is that their policies are based on false principles, which means they are leading to evil consequences. Beyond that, our enemies have never been more corrupt, petty, stupid, and laughable.

By contrast, we have almost no real-world institutions of our own, just shifting battle-lines and outposts on the internet and social media. Our only real advantage is the truth, as well as the credibility that comes from telling it. But effective policies can only be based on reality, thus we are the only ones offering workable solutions for the problems created by multiculturalism. Beyond that, we really have the best people.

Fighting a political battle means pitting our greatest weaknesses against the enemy's greatest strength. That is a losing strategy. Fighting a metapolitical battle, however, means using our greatest strengths to attack where the enemy is weakest. Only after attaining broad metapolitical hegemony will we be able to muster the resources to take control of actual institutions.

This analysis has forced me to confront a contradiction in my own thinking. I have long maintained that White Nationalism will never triumph until it leaves the Right-wing ghetto and becomes the common sense of the whole political spectrum. There needs to be a racially-conscious Right, a racially-conscious center, and a racially-conscious Left, and we know this is possible, since such things have already existed throughout the white world. For instance, America's Asian exclusion movement, South African Apartheid, and the White Australia policy were all supported by the racially-conscious Left.

Nevertheless, I am quite comfortable in the Right-wing ghetto. Honesty compels me to be a man of the Right, since I believe that there are values higher than equality and individual liberty.

But although I am a man of the Right, *I am not a Right-wing sectarian.* I want the White Nationalist idea to leave the Right-wing ghetto and redefine the whole political spectrum. Right-wing sectarians, however, seek to confine White Nationalism to ever narrower reaches of the far Right.

Right-wing sectarianism is a self-marginalizing, self-defeating tendency, and it could not come at a worse time, for the historical moment has never been more receptive to white identity politics. More people are looking to us for answers than ever before. We must develop new platforms, spokesmen, and messages to try reach and convert every white group: every age group, every social class, every religion, every ethnic group, every interest group, every subculture—everyone. This is how white identity politics will attain complete cultural and political hegemony. But instead of outreach, the movement is turning inward.

The problem started in the fall of 2016, just before Trump was elected, with the Alt Right "brand" war. Large numbers of half-baked civic nationalists and cultural libertarians suddenly started calling themselves "Alt Right," because they supported Trump and wanted to distance themselves from movement conservatism. I saw this as an opportunity to embrace, not a threat to repulse. After all, you can only convert people to White Nationalism who aren't *already* White Nationalists, and you can only convert them if they are willing to listen to you. And, for a time, they were willing to listen.

The Alt Right "brand" was a White Nationalist entryist and outreach project from the very start. But the Alt Right worked best for White Nationalists by not being exclusively associated with White Nationalism. Normies would never try the Alt Right on for size if it were an exclusively White Nationalist movement, much less associated with people like Nazis and the KKK. The Left, of course, understands the power of such associations to freeze thought and action on the Right, which is why Leftists trot them out time and again.

Some White Nationalists, however, were more concerned with exerting control over a "brand" than outreach to the public. So they hit on the same tactic as the

ADL, SPLC, and mainstream media: to chase people away from the Alt Right by associating it with Nazis and the KKK. The best example of this is the troll campaign against Steven Crowder, who made the mistake of calling himself Alt Right and was rewarded with a storm of memes in which he was welcomed to the ranks of Nazi extremists. It was hilarious, vicious stuff, but completely self-defeating from the point of view of outreach and conversion.

After Hailgate, the Alt Right was forever identified not just with White Nationalism, but with Nazism. This led to a split between the Alt Right and the Alt Lite.

The Alt Lite consists of civic nationalists who are explicitly opposed to white identity politics. Instead, it is the Right-wing identity politics of white race-mixers, non-whites, and diaspora Jews.

The Alt Right has increasingly adopted the ideas, images, and ethos of neo-Nazis and White Nationalism 1.0 (e.g., skinheads and the National Alliance) and is rife with purges and schisms as different factions seek to create a smaller, weaker, dumber, and more "pure" movement.

Both Alt Right and Alt Lite are at each other's throats, but they do have one major thing in common. They are equally incompatible with white identity politics breaking out of the margins and redefining the cultural and political mainstream, which is precisely how I define victory.

Counter-Currents, August 4, 2017

REDEFINING THE MAINSTREAM

This is the text of my talk from the Scandza Forum in Stockholm on April 7, 2018.

How can white identity politics make its way from the margins to the mainstream? There are two things we can do to make our ideas more mainstream. We can change their substance, or we can change their style, i.e., the way we communicate them. Obviously, it is self-defeating to change our beliefs to fit the mainstream. Indeed, the whole point of our movement is to change the mainstream to fit our beliefs. But although our core principles should be fixed and non-negotiable, we should be willing to be quite suave, supple, and pragmatic in the means by which we communicate them if we hope to convince the largest possible number of our people.

White identity politics has the best chance of winning if it breaks out of the Right-wing ghetto to which it is confined today and becomes the common sense of the entire cultural and political mainstream. If the legitimacy of white identity politics permeates the entire culture, the political realm will inevitably fall into line.

This political realignment can take place in two ways, exemplified by contemporary Poland and Hungary. In Poland's 2015 national parliamentary elections, a number of Left-wing parties participated, but none of them got above the threshold for representation, so the Left ended up with zero seats in the parliament. In Hungary, by contrast, Leftist parties have some seats in the parliament, but even Left-wing Hungarians tend to be patriotic and sensible on issues of immigration and diversity.

For instance, Gyula Thürmer, the leader of the tiny orthodox Marxist-Leninist Magyar Munkáspárt (Hungarian Workers' Party), stated in an interview that the party opposed taking migrants and refugees from the Middle East because they would harm Hungarian workers and increase social disharmony by adding diversity.[1] When the far Left and the far Right are united on issues connected with immigration and identity, whites need not fear political pluralism.

But whether political success follows the Polish or the Hungarian model, the aim of our movement today should be the same: to persuade as many of our people as possible of the legitimacy of white identity politics. We need to convince whites of every class, every educational level, every religious denomination, every shade of the ideological and political spectrum, and every subculture (right down to the Trekkies) that white identity politics is morally legitimate, practically feasible, and necessary for securing the things they love.

Obviously, the best apostles we can send to convert these different groups will be drawn from their ranks, since their target audiences can better identify with them. Thus we need to convert white identitarians of all shades and stripes and send them forth to set up platforms and communicate our message to others of their kind. We need to colonize every niche in the cultural and political ecosystem with custom-tailored pro-white messages, if we wish to convert as many people as possible.

So what can we do to accomplish this? A deeper question, though, is: Do we need to do anything at all—anything different from what we are already doing? After all, the existing White Nationalist movement was not created and guided by some mastermind. Instead, it coalesced out of many independent voices that created platforms for themselves or colonized existing ones.

---

[1] Interview with Gyula Thürmer of the Hungarian Workers' Party, *Counter-Currents*, April 6, 2018.

Moreover, the growth of our movement has far more to do with the failures of multiculturalism than our own efforts at propaganda and organization. Events are arguing in our favor better than we are. Even if we do nothing, the same forces driving the rise of white identity politics might well break them out of the Right-wing ghetto and change the cultural and political mainstream in the same unplanned and decentralized manner.

But wouldn't it be nice if we could give this process some intelligent guidance? Wouldn't it be nice if we could network and cooperate with some of these emerging voices and platforms and organizations? Some benefits of cooperation include:

- ❖ learning from the experiences—and mistakes—of others
- ❖ not wasting scarce resources duplicating the efforts and competing with the events and products of other nationalists. We need cartelization, not destructive competition.
- ❖ adjudicating disputes in an equitable—and quiet—manner, or avoiding them altogether
- ❖ perhaps even collaborating with one another to accomplish tasks too great to accomplish on one's own

To make such cooperation possible, we simply have to learn to work with people who share our views of white identity politics but may not share our views on a whole range of other issues. And as our movement grows more successful in penetrating and changing the whole culture, it will eventually be the case that white identity politics might be the *only* thing that unites us.

Of course we will continue to have passionate opinions and disagreements on other topics. But we need to be willing to set these aside to work with others for the greater good of our race. That one simple trick is the key to ensuring the broadest possible cooperation and coordination among white advocates, creating a movement that is larger, more powerful, and more likely to be able to save our race.

By contrast, people who insist on combining White Nationalism with a list of Right-wing add-ons—who try to up-sell you a side dish of Orthodox Christianity, or Nordic paganism, or radical Traditionalism with your ethnoburger—who insist that these peripheral issues are essential to white preservationism, and who turn them into polarizing litmus tests and shibboleths, are guaranteed to create a smaller, weaker, dumber, poorer, and less effective—but more "pure"—movement, when we need to go in precisely the opposite direction.

Such behavior is often dismissed as "purity spiraling." But purity is not a problem. The problem is failing to distinguish between what is essential and what is peripheral to white identity politics. We should keep our core principles pure. The mistake is to demand purity on marginal matters as well.

There is a difference between a political ideology and a political movement. A political ideology is defined by its first principles. A political movement is defined by its goals. It is possible for people to share the same political goals for a wide variety of ideological reasons. Insisting that we all have the same reasons is the source of sectarianism.

If our movement is to grow, we need to discourage such sectarian tendencies. Currently they are of the Right, because that's where our movement began. But Left-wing sectarianism will inevitably emerge as our movement grows to encompass the whole political spectrum.

The best defense against sectarianism is to recognize the symptoms and check them when they appear in ourselves and others. We need to see sectarianism with an accurately jaundiced eye.

- ❖ Sectarianism is a sign of ignorance that needs to be corrected.
- ❖ Sectarianism is a sign of immaturity that needs to be outgrown.
- ❖ Sectarianism is a manifestation of what I call "honorable defeatism,"[2] which is a self-defeating behavior pattern that can be discerned in education, employment, personal relationships, and politics. If a person is convinced that defeat is inevitable, he will no longer seek victory. Instead, he will seek to preserve his self-esteem by finding an honorable, face-saving excuse for defeat. He will also seek to preserve his sense of agency by taking defeat into his own hands. Thus he will defeat himself on a matter of high moral principle. Of course it is never so blatant as that. Honorable defeatism may be perfectly obvious to others, but it only works if you are not fully conscious of what you are doing. So learning to distrust your own inclination towards moralism goes a long way to suppressing this problem altogether.
- ❖ Sectarianism is exactly what the enemy would encourage in order to retard, disintegrate, and defeat our movement. We should never accuse people of being enemy agents without rock-solid proof. But we should have no hesitation to call out those who *act like* them.
- ❖ Sectarianism is a tired tactic of would-be

---

[2] Greg Johnson, "Honorable Defeatists," *In Defense of Prejudice.*

movement "leaders" to build up their own
brand or grouplet, to avenge themselves on
their enemies, or to gain advantages over their
rivals at the expense of the health and growth
of the larger movement. We need to call them
on it, every time.

If we train ourselves to spot the slightest sectarian
tendencies, sigh disdainfully, and mutter "This again,"
the problem will be significantly reduced.

But can we stamp out divisive and sectarian behavior
altogether? Not really. We can't expel people from a decentralized, largely online movement. Trying to bully
people offline is a dumb idea, because whether you win
or lose depends entirely on the decision of your enemy,
which is not the sort of battle that intelligent men fight.
Besides, there is really no way to keep a motivated person "off the internet." But we can and should bar divisive
types from our membership organizations and online
platforms. We can't prevent them from marginalizing
themselves, but we can sure prevent them from marginalizing us.

Aside from keeping sectarian types at arm's length, all
we can do is call them out on their bad behavior and
hope that they grow out of it. Then we need to get back
to work. The best criticism, after all, is simply to do better work, knowing that it will accomplish more and attract the most perceptive and sensible people. So focus-
ing too much on sectarian cranks with their sandwich-
boards is itself a self-defeating distraction.

We also need to be realistic. In a growing movement
there will always be fresh crops of the ignorant, imma-
ture, and self-defeating. But that's actually a good problem to have. We want the movement to grow, so it will
always be necessary to educate and assimilate newcomers. It would be nice if the world simply handed us disci-

plined political soldiers to work with. But we have to create them ourselves. This sort of education is what metapolitics is all about. Moreover, if the supply of new sectarian types magically dried up, the enemy would find it necessary to create them. Thus we will never be free of this plague, but we can reduce it, contain it, work around it, and, most importantly, figure out how we can win in spite of it.

Does the decision to set aside differences to unite the broadest possible coalition around advancing the idea of white identity politics imply that politics is our highest value, trumping religion, family, private life, etc.?

Yes and no.

On the yes side, I see nothing wrong with proposing that the center pole of our political "big tent" be white identity politics. What is wrong with making a political goal the highest value of an eminently political movement?

No, to the extent that politics is not the sole realm of values or life. You may place religion, family, and your personal life above politics. In fact, I hope you do. Not everyone can be a one-dimensional ideologue like me.

But, again, this is a political movement. Our political goals must come first, and the inessential issues that divide us must be set aside, so we can argue about them in the ethnostate. Because if we argue about them now, we will never get to the ethnostate.

We do have to be frank, though, that this "big tent" approach implies that a certain "liberal" tolerance will be an ingredient in our movement and thus will be "baked in" to the ethnostates we are going to create. For instance, if the movement tables religious differences, that means that religious pluralism will be built into our movement today and into our ethnostates tomorrow. Thus if people enter the movement with the aim of establishing some sort of religious theocracy, they are joining under false pretenses, hoping to trick people into fighting for a form of society in which they have no place. The same is true of such shibboleths as libertarian economics, "white *sharia*," and murdering homosexuals. No sensible person will join a movement or a party if he suspects such hidden sectarian agendas.

Combating sectarianism should not be confused with a complete ban on criticism and debate in the movement. As I argue in my articles on the absurd attempt to create a taboo against "punching right,"[3] criticism and debate are the lifeblood of a pluralistic metapolitical movement. But there's a difference between constructive and destructive criticism. For instance, sectarianism makes our movement weaker. But criticizing sectarianism makes us stronger. We need to stop arguing about inessential matters, so we can argue about essential ones.

Many in our movement envision our path to victory on the Old Right model of a militant, hierarchical political party using both bullets and ballots to battle its way to power and then impose its program on society. But the conquest of political power has metapolitical conditions. At least some people *outside* the movement need to regard its aims as morally legitimate and politically feasible before it can hold a single rally or win a single vote. Those among us who regard politics as simply a matter of hard political power put themselves in the place of an invading army or Leninist vanguard party imposing an unpopular revolution by force of arms.

The more people who agree with a party's aims, the less opposition it will face. This is obviously true of its natural Right-wing constituency. But it also applies more broadly—in fact, to the entire electorate. Opposition to our politics will decrease as its moral legitimacy increas-

---

[3] Greg Johnson, "Punching Right," *In Defense of Prejudice* and "Punching Right 2," next in this volume.

es throughout the whole of society. But what if our ideas become the common sense of the whole political spectrum? We know that this is possible, because it was actual not so long ago.

If we work hard enough to convert our people, there may come a point when it no longer makes sense to conceive of victory as the triumph of a particular party, because on the essential issues of white identity politics, all the parties will be on the same page. Just as every mainstream party today is on the same page about diversity and multiculturalism.

Such a consensus would transcend any particular political party and thus would have to be institutionalized outside or above the political realm. We need a network of metapolitical organizations to set and monitor the boundaries of political discourse. When people today speak of an "establishment" or a "deep state," they are gesturing toward such agents of ideological hegemony.

In such a society, white identity politics would be the uncontested framework of the political mainstream. For those who are fixated on a particular Right-wing sectarian vision of society, this might seem like defeat. But a society in which white people—and only white people— are arguing about the same old political issues, like abortion, environmentalism, and taxes, is victory enough for me.

Counter-Currents, April 9, 2018

PUNCHING RIGHT 2

In my essay "Punching Right"[1] I explained why I think that there should not be any taboos against criticizing fellow Right-wingers. The only taboos should be against bad ideas, bad arguments, bad manners, and bad faith.

In this essay I want to criticize two false assumptions of those who would make punching Right into a taboo. Punching Right is supposed to be a sin because:

- ❖ All criticisms of the far Right from the mainstream Right are cowardly, dishonest, and perhaps venal, because the critics secretly agree with the far Right.
- ❖ The Left is dominant because it always presents a united front and never punches Left. If we Rightists want to win, therefore, we must never punch Right.

Both of these ideas are false.

First, not all of us on the Right agree with each other. We are not all on the "same side." The very idea of a political spectrum fosters the illusion that if two schools of thought are both on the Right, they must be just two versions of the same thing, differing only in matters of degree. But of course Right and Left are on the same political spectrum as well, and we do not think they differ only in degree.

Political philosophies differ fundamentally in terms of their basic principles and their political goals. This is true of Left vs. Right, and it is true of one Right vs. another. The only thing that really unites the different camps of

---

[1] Greg Johnson, "Punching Right," *In Defense of Prejudice*.

the Right is a negative belief, namely rejecting the idea that equality is the highest political value. (The camps of the Left are more unified because they all affirm a positive, namely that equality is the highest political value.)

I will grant that different tendencies on the Right might share certain specific policy goals and certain specific enemies. Thus they might find it expedient to band together for common defense or common goals. But that does not mean that they share the same ultimate ideological principles or the same ultimate political goals.

Under some circumstances, it is pragmatic to agree to disagree. But when those circumstances no longer hold, people will inevitably air their differences. And there is absolutely nothing wrong with that. If you are unwilling to discuss what you believe and what you want, specifically with people who *disagree* with you, *you are never going to persuade new people to your side.* But in a war of ideas, persuasion is fighting and conversion is victory.

Why does a taboo on punching Right assume that our opponents secretly agree with us? Those who punch Right either agree with us or they disagree with us. If they disagree with us, we might have a long list of reasons why we think they are wrong. But we have no basis to criticize them simply for *voicing* their disagreements. After all, stating your principles and defending them is the only intellectually honest and honorable course available.

Thus we can only really object to those who "punch Right" if they secretly agree with us but nevertheless attack us out of cowardice, dishonesty, and ulterior motives, such as the pursuit of money and social status. Thus there is nothing inherently wrong about "punching Right." It is only wrong if it springs from base motives.

But how many people are we talking about here? And how do we know who they are?

For the sake of argument, let's stipulate that White

Nationalism is not just an inherently Right-wing position, but the most radical Right-wing position possible. I think both of those views are in fact false, but that is a topic for another article.

Now let's ask ourselves what is the likely proportion of our critics who sincerely disagree with us on matters of principle vs. those who secretly really agree with us. Realistically speaking, what percentage of people on the Right as a whole agree with White Nationalism? I think that number falls somewhere between 1 and 5%. Anything more is flattering or fooling ourselves.

Let's be exuberant and say that 5% of Rightists agree with us. Now, of that 5%, what percentage do you think is likely to attack us out of base motives while secretly agreeing with us? Is it even one in a hundred—1% of 5%? If so, then the injunction not to punch Right actually applies to almost nobody. On the Right, 95% of people disagree with us in good faith, 5% agree with us, and a minuscule percentage of those dishonestly criticize us anyway. By these rough calculations, *punching Right is almost never wrong.*

And how do we distinguish those who punch Right from dishonest motives from the vast majority of people who sincerely disagree with us? Short of a confession, we are forced to divine people's motives from their external behavior, and that is sometimes a difficult task.

Thus, given how minuscule and gnat-sized the number of people who punch Right in bad faith must be, and given how difficult it is to really fathom the motives of others, one would expect to very seldom hear the accusation that "X secretly agrees with us but is betraying us out of base motives." But of course, given the prominence of the "paranoid style" in our movement—paranoids always fear the worst and jump to conclusions—*we hear such accusations all the time.* But throwing around such accusations is like hunting a gnat with a blunderbuss. It seldom hits the gnat, but the scattershot certainly clears the room of innocent bystanders.

If almost nobody punches Right out of base motives, and if we can almost never be sure about human motives in the first place, the most pragmatic course is simply to drop speculations about motives entirely and to try to persuade our critics that we have better facts and arguments than they do. If our critics are not honest men, we will never persuade them, of course, but we will probably persuade the most honest among the onlookers. And bringing honest people to our side—as opposed to denouncing and extirpating the evils we imagine lurking in the hearts of a very tiny percentage of our enemies—is the most important thing to do anyway.

Of course it would seem quite convenient if we could persuade our critics that it is taboo to oppose us. For instance, many of us would be delighted if moderates would accept Jonathan Bowden's recommendation that they treasure the extremists to their Right and draw upon their ideas and energy.

But this is never going to happen, because ultimately *White Nationalists believe and want very different things than the civic nationalists, classical liberals, neoconservatives, and Christian conservatives who oppose us.* They have different philosophies and goals. They don't want to be like us. They have nothing to gain from us—except looking more moderate and reasonable to centrist eyes, which is really the only reason they mention us at all.

Our enemies will never be fooled by a taboo on punching Right. But even if they did accept it, it would actually harm our cause. Again, we are in a war of ideas. If our goal is to convert people to our way of thinking, we need to promote open intellectual debate not taboos that shut it down. We can't change people's minds if we don't even know what they think and why.

Again, there are circumstances in which it makes

sense to agree to disagree so we can focus on common concrete goals. But we can't defer debate about fundamental differences of principles and goals forever, and the desire to do so probably springs from a failure to take ideas seriously at all.

Second, the idea that Leftists are winning because they never fight among themselves does not stand up to the slightest historical scrutiny. Tell it to Trotsky. Within the Marxist camp, political disagreements were intense enough to lead to mass murder. The Cold War was between two different versions of Leftist ideology. Marxism is illiberal, and liberalism is anti-totalitarian, yet both ideologies are Leftist. Far from being threatened by principled intellectual disagreement, the Left has been willing to court global thermonuclear war over ideology. They take ideas seriously.

Again, the idea of a political spectrum fosters the illusion that all Leftist outlooks differ only in degree, and that John Kennedy or Hillary Clinton have the same ultimate goals as Herbert Marcuse or Chairman Mao. Leftists do prize equality above other political values, but that leaves a wide latitude for passionate and bloody disagreements about what the best society is and why.

The illusion that Leftists stand united and do not disavow their more extremist elements is fostered by both the Leftist media and the cuckservative Right, which routinely demand that conservatives denounce people to their Right but of course spare liberals the same necessity.

When Donald Trump disavowed the Alt Right or David Duke, he was only being honest. After all, he really does disagree with us. What is objectionable is that Hillary Clinton was never asked to disavow the support of Black Lives Matter thugs or a murderer like Donna Hylton, and Barack Obama was never made to answer questions about Bill Ayres or Jeremiah Wright. Both Rachel Maddow and John McCain agree that such questions would be "unfair," for it should go without saying that liberals never support bad things. But if Clinton or Obama were put on the spot and asked to distance themselves from their most unsavory supporters, I have no doubt that they would disavow them, and they might even be sincere.

If the secret of the Left's success isn't a matter of never "punching Left," then what is it? The Left has many genuine strengths, including greater moral seriousness and psychological intensity.[2] But a big part of the Left's success is simply the lack of an effective Right-wing opposition. We will be a lot more effective if we stop being threatened by principled intellectual disagreement and start taking ideas a bit more seriously.

Counter-Currents, July 17, 2017

---

[2] See Greg Johnson, "Metapolitics and Occult Warfare," "The Moral Factor," and "Learning from the Left," in *New Right vs. Old Right* (San Francisco: Counter-Currents, 2013).

BEYOND THE ALT RIGHT:
TOWARD A NEW NATIONALISM

The Alt Right is dead. But the Alt Right was so useful—and so much fun—that we need to create a replacement for it, the sooner the better.

By the Alt Right, I mean the online movement of White Nationalist podcasters, bloggers, and social media trolls that emerged in 2014, coalesced around the Trump candidacy in 2015, then began to change the parameters of political debate with stinging memes like the "cuckservative" barb, becoming an international media phenomenon in 2016.

As I argue in my essay "What is the Alternative Right?" (above) this new Alt Right was quite different from the original Alt Right that took its name from the *Alternative Right* webzine which Richard Spencer founded in 2010 and edited until 2012. The two Alt Rights differed in terms of ethos, intellectual influences, and preferred platforms and media, although they did come to share an ideology and a name. By the beginning of 2015, the new Alt Right was increasingly comfortable with White Nationalism as an ideology and the Alt Right as a brand.

Aside from the fact that #AltRight made a good hashtag, the main utility of the term was its vagueness. It allowed people to signal their dissent from mainstream Republicanism without embracing such stigmatized labels as National Socialism and White Nationalism. The Alt Right was thus an ideal "discursive space" in which White Nationalists could interact with, influence, and convert people who were closer to the political mainstream.

White Nationalists should always remember how we came to our views. We should never lose sight of the fact that it takes an inner struggle, ended by an act of courage, to seriously consider heretical and highly stigmatized ideas, even online, in the privacy of one's own home. Thus we need safe spaces for trying on new ideas and building new relationships. The Alt Right provided that. It allowed people to experiment with being radical and edgy without being one of "those people" or burning one's bridges to the mainstream.

The result was a grassroots online insurgency mobilizing a vast network of highly creative individuals and injecting their memes and talking points into the mainstream, where they began shifting popular consciousness and political debates.

But, as I argued in "What Is the Alternative Right?," the Alt Right's success in attracting people led to a crisis. Both versions of the Alt Right were always, at core, White Nationalist outreach projects. But there was a perennial battle in the Alt Right between the people who advocated a "big tent" movement and the "purity spiralers" and Right-wing sectarians who wanted to enforce one ideological orthodoxy or another.

I was in the big tent camp. I argued that outreach projects by their nature attract people who do not (yet) agree with us. But you can only convert people who don't already agree with you. The whole point of the movement was to convert rather than repel people who disagreed with us.

But the new Alt Right was such a successful outreach project that it was being flooded with large numbers of Trumpian civic nationalists, including non-whites, who rejected White Nationalism. I thought this was more of an opportunity than a crisis, and that we needed to take a deep breath, remind ourselves that truth is on our side, and then get back to the battle of ideas. Others, however, became concerned that the Alt Right brand would be hijacked or coopted by civic nationalists like Milo Yiannopoulos. This was the Alt Right "brand war" of the fall of 2016.

The brand war came to an end with the Hailgate incident of November 21, 2016, when, before the cameras of the enemy media, Richard Spencer raised his glass with the words "Hail Trump, Hail our People, Hail Victory!" and people in the audience responded with Nazi salutes. This stunt indelibly identified the Alt Right not just with White Nationalism but with neo-Nazism in the minds of the whole world.[1]

This led to a split between White Nationalists and civic nationalists, who came to be called the Alt Lite. To differentiate itself from the Alt Right, the Alt Lite dug in its heels on the one issue that White Nationalists most urgently need to destroy: the moral taboo against white identity politics. The great big beautiful tent, where civic nationalism and ethnonationalism could be debated—an argument that White Nationalists always win—was replaced by a great big ugly wall, over which only venomous Tweet barrages were exchanged.

The expanding discursive space in which White Nationalists could influence the mainstream was replaced by a self-marginalizing political sect which in 2017 began to focus on street activism, even though they were vastly outnumbered and outgunned by the Left, which could count on collaborators in the media and all levels of government, as well as armies of lawyers and effectively unlimited funds. White Nationalists have none of these advantages. Thus a movement that had grown by attacking the system's moral and intellectual weaknesses from a position of strength was replaced by a movement that attacked the system's institutional power centers from a position of weakness. Catastrophic failure was inevitable.

By the end of 2017, much of the American White Nationalist movement was simply exhausted from the wave

---

[1] See Greg Johnson, "The Alt Right: Obituary for a Brand?" in *In Defense of Prejudice.*

of doxings, deplatforming, and lawfare that followed the Unite the Right rally in Charlottesville, Virginia, on August 12, 2017. In the days following Unite the Right, more than one hundred people disappeared from my social media sphere alone. They obviously did not change their political convictions, but they clearly believed that the movement was going the wrong direction. Nevertheless, the rallies and college speaking events continued, hemorrhaging people and money—which were in short supply to begin with—until they finally bled out.

The post-mortem of the activist phase of the Alt Right led to a healthy debate about "optics" and whether it is better for American White Nationalists to embrace American political traditions and symbols or imported ones.[2] There was also a growing consensus that the movement needed to return to our strengths, namely the war of ideas. Even activist events needed to be reconfigured along the lines of the European Identitarian movement, which does not battle antifa but engages in low-risk, high-reward publicity stunts, i.e., "propaganda of the deed."[3]

But for many in the American movement, 2018 has simply been a year of watching and waiting. People hunkered down to let the storm pass. Now that it is dying down, they are surveying the damage and wondering what comes next.

Wouldn't it be nice to have a common cause to rally around again? Wouldn't it be nice to have a new discursive space in which we could again interface with and perhaps influence the political mainstream?

Some people are hoping that Trump's re-election campaign might provide a rallying point, but most of us have

---

[2] See Greg Johnson, "Is White Nationalism Un-American?" and "What is American Nationalism?" above.

[3] See Greg Johnson, "Interview on Unite the Right 1 and 2," above.

lost our enthusiasm for Trump. Thankfully, there's something bigger and better than Trump. While there will always be a place for defending Trump's National Populist policies from critics and detractors, we can't lose sight of the big picture. We need to look beyond Trump to the forces that made Trump possible.

These are the same forces behind the Brexit victory; behind the rise of politicians like Viktor Orbán, Matteo Salvini, and Sebastian Kurz; behind the success of parties like Alternative for Germany, Poland's Law and Justice, and the Sweden Democrats; and behind the Yellow Vests insurgency in France.

All of these are manifestations of what is called National Populism or the New Nationalism. We need to understand the forces driving the rise of the New Nationalism. Then we need to add our impetus to these forces and try to steer them toward White Nationalism. The New Nationalism should be our new rallying point, our new discursive space in which we can inject our ideas into mainstream discussions.

For starters, I urge every White Nationalist to read *National Populism: The Revolt Against Liberal Democracy* by Roger Eatwell and Matthew Goodwin,[4] two British political scientists specializing in populism and political extremism.

Eatwell and Goodwin are evidently men of the Left, but they do not seem to be liberals or globalists. Indeed, they relish demolishing liberal and globalist illusions about National Populism, arguing that it cannot be dismissed as mere fascism or racism; nor can it be dismissed as simply a flash in the pan, the product of ephemeral events like the 2008 recession or the migrant crisis; nor is it the last

---

4 Roger Eatwell and Matthew Goodwin, *National Populism: The Revolt Against Liberal Democracy* (New York: Pelican, 2018).

hurrah of "old white males" who will soon die off and be replaced by tolerant Millennials; nor, finally, is it merely the product of charismatic politicians.

Instead, Eatwell and Goodwin argue that National Populism is the product of deep social and political trends which they call the four Ds: Distrust, Destruction, Deprivation, and De-Alignment. *Distrust* refers to the breakdown of popular trust in political elites. *Destruction* primarily means destruction of identity, i.e., the destruction of peoples and cultures by immigration and multiculturalism. National Populism is, therefore, a form of white identity politics. *Deprivation* means the erosion of First World middle-class and working-class living standards due to globalization and neoliberalism. *De-Alignment* is the breakdown of voter identification with dominant political parties.

Eatwell and Goodwin marshal impressive empirical studies that indicate that these trends are pervasive in white countries. These trends are also deep-seated rather than ephemeral. Not only are they going to continue on into the future, they are likely to grow stronger before they abate. Thus, National Populism is here to stay. National Populism is the wave of the future, not just a ripple in the news cycle (hence the great wave on the cover of their book). Eatwell and Goodwin are so confident of this that in their final chapter, "Towards Post-Populism," the only post-populist scenario they can imagine is the political establishment adopting National Populist policies. In other words, they think National Populism will likely become the hegemonic political outlook. This is an astonishing concession, since it means that the hegemony of globalism is drawing to a close.

I find this analysis deeply encouraging, and it puts to rest a fear that has been gnawing at me for the last two years. I believe that nothing less than White Nationalism can save our race, thus the success of our movement is the supreme moral imperative. Whites are in a state of emergency. This is *serious*. This is *urgent*. Thus in 2015 and 2016, I was thrilled to see forces in the broader political realm aligning with White Nationalist ideas and goals, specifically Brexit and the Trump phenomenon.

But I also thought it likely that this historical moment would be fleeting. Thus we had to capitalize on it while it was still possible. This is why I was so horrified at Hailgate, when instead of giving a statesmanlike speech outlining how the National Policy Institute would serve as the intellectual vanguard for National Populism—a move that would have secured Spencer's bid for movement leadership and attracted significant resources—he instead chose the path of juvenile buffoonery, hoping to ingratiate himself with the cool kids at *The Right Stuff* and on the chans.

But that was just the beginning of months of sectarianism, schisms, purges, and purity spirals. In 2017, we saw the birth of toxic, self-marginalizing memes like "white *sharia*" and the return of the worst ideas and attitudes of White Nationalism 1.0. We had arrived at a moment of decision, and our "leaders" had chosen juvenility and irrelevance. They were not ready for prime time. As I explained in my essay "Against Right-Wing Sectarianism" (above), this could only lead to a smaller, weaker, poorer, and dumber movement. Such a movement would be unable to halt white genocide.

By May of 2017, I started thinking that we needed a new "brand." The term "New Nationalism" was already being used to describe National Populism. The term was broad and vague enough to encompass everyone from White Nationalists to sitting presidents and ruling parties. I even went so far as to reserve the domain name newnationalism.net. In keeping with my essay "Redefining the Mainstream" (above), I envisioned a discursive space that was the exact opposite of Right-wing sectarianism. Our movement must prefigure the hegemony we want to create in the broader society, encompassing the full diversity of whites, united only by the central principle of white identity politics and free to differ on all other matters.

The most important intellectual battle is over the *legitimacy* of white identity politics. The greatest political taboo of our times is the idea that identity politics is immoral for white people—and *only* for white people. This taboo unites the whole political establishment against us. The political establishment knows this, but many National Populists don't. This is why the establishment attacks National Populists as fascists, nativists, and racists.

But many National Populists don't challenge the idea that white identity politics is immoral. Instead, they insist that they are color-blind civic nationalists, concerned only with a common culture. Then they try to turn the tables on Leftism and accuse it of being *the real identity politics*.

But, of course, the Left is not going to drop identity politics. Why would they drop a winning strategy? Foreswearing identity politics is a losing strategy for the Right, akin to unilateral disarmament, taking a knife to a gunfight, or allowing one's opponents a trump card but refusing to use it oneself.[5]

Thus, the New Nationalism platform needed to be a space where one could argue about virtually anything *except* the moral legitimacy of white identity politics. Instead, our overriding editorial agenda would be to establish that white identity politics is inevitable, necessary, and moral—and to expose the moral illegitimacy of the system.

I shared this idea with a number of writers, podcasters, and video bloggers who also believed the Alt Right was spiraling into irrelevance. They were uniformly enthusias-

---

[5] See Greg Johnson, "Why Conservatives Conserve Nothing," reprinted above, and "In the Short Run," in *The White Nationalist Manifesto*.

tic. But there were things I had to take care of first, like finishing *The White Nationalist Manifesto*. I also sensed that it would be some time before the Alt Right would finally exhaust itself and people would be ready for something new. Eventually, though, I decided that I want to stick with *Counter-Currents*. I still think that a *New Nationalism* webzine is a good idea. But somebody else needs to create it.

Of course White Nationalists do not need a new platform to contribute to the rise of National Populism. In fact, we have been contributing to it for quite some time. Furthermore, if Eatwell and Goodwin are right, we will be contributing to it well into the future, for white nations will be receptive to National Populism for some time to come. And although nothing has greater *moral urgency* than stopping white genocide, we've got time to get our message and our strategies right. (And if we don't have time to do it right, doing it wrong won't save us, anyway.)

So, how can White Nationalists insert ourselves into the broader National Populist phenomenon? Let's look at Eatwell and Goodwin's four Ds again.

Distrust: When people distrust their rulers, the system loses legitimacy and power. White Nationalists are masterful at mocking the lies, hypocrisy, sanctimony, cowardice, and degeneracy of our rulers. Furthermore, nothing destroys trust in the establishment quite like learning that its ultimate agenda is the genocide of the white race.[6]

But our propaganda needs to be truthful as well, because we want people to trust us. For if distrust becomes pervasive throughout society, then the people cannot unite against the establishment. Our goal is to promote a high-trust society. We cannot accomplish that if we cynically resort to lies because "That's what the establishment

---

[6] See Greg Johnson, "White Genocide," in *The White Nationalist Manifesto*.

does to us." If we want to replace the establishment, we have to be better than the establishment.

Destruction: White Nationalists have been raising awareness of the destruction of white nations and cultures through immigration and multiculturalism for decades. Even so, our educational efforts have awakened far fewer people than the negative consequences of immigration and multiculturalism themselves. The system is doing far more to *push* people toward white identity politics than we are doing to *pull* them. Thus, white racial consciousness will continue to rise even if our movement is completely censored.

We should, of course, do everything we can to raise awareness. But I think we have a much more important role to play, namely *deepening* awareness.

First, we need to help people understand *why* multiculturalism is a failure—namely, racial and ethnic diversity in the same state is always a source of weakness[7]—so we don't waste our time with half-measures like "conservative" multicultural civic nationalism. Moreover, only White Nationalists fully understand the forces promoting mass migrations and multiculturalism and how they fit into the overall agenda of white genocide.

Second, and most importantly, we need to defend the *moral legitimacy* of white identity politics. Vast numbers of whites are in thrall to the establishment because they believe there is something immoral about taking their own side in ethnic conflicts. This taboo is like a dam, holding back the floodwaters of National Populism. Once we break that dam, the wave of National Populism will sweep away the whole rotten system.

Deprivation: Basic economics predicts that globalization will lead to the collapse of middle-class and working-

---

[7] See Greg Johnson, "What's Wrong with Diversity?," in *The White Nationalist Manifesto*.

class living standards throughout the First World, although First World elites will benefit quite a lot. Obviously, the masses in any First World society never consented to such policies. Genuine Leftists recognize that globalization has undermined the gains of the Left in the First World. But global socialism is not the answer to global capitalism. Only National Populists understand the natural limit of globalization: the nation-state.[8]

De-Alignment: When voters begin to distrust the establishment, they begin to distrust establishment political parties as well. White Nationalists are masterful at showing that electoral politics, in which voters take sides in the battles between mainstream political parties, is only a superficial distraction from real politics. Political power does not lie in voters choosing between Coke and Diet Coke. That's an election that the Coca-Cola Corporation can't lose.

Real power lies in framing all political debates so that, no matter which party ends up in power, the establishment always wins. Real power lies in establishing the things about which political parties *agree rather than fight* and about which the voters are *never given a choice*.[9] The political establishment, center-Left and center-Right, is of one mind on the goodness of globalization, immigration, and multiculturalism—the very things that National Populists oppose.

What white people want is essentially a socially conservative, interventionist state. We want National Populism. What the establishment wants is socially liberal global capitalism, what Jonathan Bowden called Left-wing oligarchy. The people are never allowed to vote for Na-

---

[8] See Greg Johnson, "The End of Globalization," in *Truth, Justice, & a Nice White Country*.

[9] See Greg Johnson, "Hegemony," in *New Right vs. Old Right*.

tional Populism straight up. The center-Right packages social conservatism with neoliberal globalization. The center-Left packages the interventionist state with social degeneracy.

When the center-Right is in power, they only give the establishment what it wants: lower taxes and freer trade for the oligarchs. When the center-Left is in power, they only give the establishment what it wants: more degeneracy. The parties blame their failures on the opposition and assure their voters that the *next time* their party is at the helm, the voters will finally get what they want.

The people are placated with the illusion of political representation in elections where the establishment parties trade power. But no matter who is elected, the outcomes always drift father and farther from what the people want, namely National Populism—and closer to what the degenerate global elites want.

White Nationalists are also highly aware of how the establishment works to co-opt National Populist uprisings like the Tea Party and now, sadly, Donald Trump. For Trump has fallen into the center-Right establishment pattern of giving the oligarchs what they want (tax cuts), failing to do what the people want (a border wall), and blaming his failure on his opponents (first the establishment Republicans, now the Democrats).

In sum, White Nationalists can intensify National Populist forces and steer them toward White Nationalism by deepening the people's *Distrust* of the establishment; broadening and deepening the people's awareness of how and why globalization, immigration, and multiculturalism are leading them to *Destruction* and *Deprivation;* and creating new political possibilities by encouraging *De-Alignment* with the establishment's sham political debates and contests.

But to ride the National Populist wave, White Nationalists have to jettison certain incompatible ideological fixations.

First and foremost, we actually have to be populists. Eatwell and Goodwin also show that National Populism is not anti-democratic. National Populists want more democracy, not less. They also argue that National Populism is not fascist in its inspirations or goals, although the establishment loves nothing more than to stigmatize National Populism with such labels. We shouldn't help them. Thus those among us who sneer at populism and democracy,[10] make fetishes out of elitism and hierarchy,[11] and try to resurrect inter-war fascist movements[12] are not helping.

Second, National Populists really are economic interventionists. Old habits die hard, but those among us who still think in terms of "free market" economics are not helping. Eatwell and Goodwin point out that in the United States, Republican voters are significantly more interventionist than Republican legislators. Which means that Koch-funded free-market fundamentalism has simply produced a party headed by ideologues who are out of touch with their constituency. Don't be one of them.

Where do we go from here? The most important thing to keep in mind is that National Populism is arising out of the *breakdown* of the political system. Just like shattering an atom, the breakdown of a system releases immense energies. It also creates radical new possibilities, "holes in being" where new actions can take place and new orders can emerge.

But the breakdown of systems also creates uncertainty and surprises. It is not an environment in which one can

---

[10] Greg Johnson, "Notes on Populism, Elitism, and Democracy" in *New Right vs. Old Right*.

[11] Greg Johnson, Introduction, in *Truth, Justice, & a Nice White Country*.

[12] Greg Johnson, "The Relevance of the Old Right," in *The White Nationalist Manifesto*.

expect to unfold grand plans. Thus, the more our movement is tied to long-term plans and fixed ideas, the less adapted we are to the climate we wish to create, and the more brittle and susceptible to catastrophic failure we become. Accordingly, at the present moment, the best overall strategy is not to get ahead of ourselves. We simply need to *promote chaos, but also plant the seeds of a new order*. Then we need to wait.

The Yellow Vests insurgency is a genuine grassroots National Populist movement. But it was nobody's grand design. It emerged spontaneously, and it surprised everyone. But spontaneous movements of large numbers of people are only possible because the participants share common views and values. Such movements also propagate through existing social networks. Thus, if we want more National Populist insurgencies, we need to promote chaos in the system, seed people's minds with models of genuine National Populist alternatives, and build real-world social networks through which we can propagate ideas and influence. Beyond that, we simply need to adopt an attitude of maximum openness and flexibility in the face of new possibilities so we can react with fresh provocations.

In short, we need more New Right metapolitics. But this is second nature to us. We've been doing it for years now. We have the best ideas, the best memes, and the best people. But we need a new focus. If Eatwell and Goodwin are right, though, we now know that we have a vast audience, strong historical winds at our back, and time enough to turn the world around. Let's make this the age of the New Nationalism.

Counter-Currents, December 21, 2018

INDEX

Numbers in bold refer to a whole chapter or section devoted to a particular topic.

ABOUT THE AUTHOR

Greg Johnson, Ph.D., is Editor-in-Chief of Counter-Currents Publishing Ltd. and the Counter-Currents.com webzine.

He is the author of nineteen books (all published by Counter-Currents, unless otherwise noted): *Confessions of a Reluctant Hater* (2010, 2016), *Trevor Lynch's White Nationalist Guide to the Movies* (2012), *New Right vs. Old Right* (2013), *Son of Trevor Lynch's White Nationalist Guide to the Movies* (2015), *Truth, Justice, & a Nice White Country* (2015), *In Defense of Prejudice* (2017), *You Asked for It: Selected Interviews*, vol. 1 (2017), *The White Nationalist Manifesto* (2018), *Toward a New Nationalism* (2019, 2023), *Return of the Son of Trevor Lynch's CENSORED Guide to the Movies* (2019), *From Plato to Postmodernism* (2019), *It's Okay to Be White: The Best of Greg Johnson* (Ministry of Truth, 2020), *Graduate School with Heidegger* (2020), *Here's the Thing: Selected Interviews*, vol. 2 (2020), *Trevor Lynch: Part Four of the Trilogy* (2020), *White Identity Politics* (2020), *The Year America Died* (2021), *Trevor Lynch's Classics of Right-Wing Cinema* (2022), and *The Trial of Socrates* (2023).

He is editor of *North American New Right*, vol. 1 (2012); *North American New Right*, vol. 2 (2017); Julius Evola, *East & West: Comparative Studies in Pursuit of Tradition* (with Collin Cleary, 2018); Francis Parker Yockey, *The Enemy of Europe* (Centennial Edition Publishing, 2022), Alain de Benoist, *Ernst Jünger: Between the Gods & the Titans* (Middle Europe Books, 2022), and many other volumes.

His writings have been translated into Arabic, Czech, Danish, Dutch, Estonian, Finnish, French, German, Greek, Hungarian, Norwegian, Polish, Portuguese, Russian, Slovak, Spanish, Swedish, and Ukrainian.